Let your taste buds lead the way with more than 170 recipes from the city's most celebrated chefs.

PRESENTED BY

MUNGENAST
LEXUS OF ST. LOUIS

plaza
LEXUS

StLouis
Chefs' Recipes

With our print publications and digital products—St. Louis Magazine,
St. Louis AT HOME, St. Louis Family, St. Louis Chefs' Recipes, Hello GoodBuy!,
and stlmag.com—SLM Media Group has built a desirable audience
within the St. Louis metropolitan area, through award-winning
editorial and design; paid, targeted circulation; signature events;
and an educated and affluent readership.

A locally owned and operated company, our informative, beautiful
publications were created to serve as the local authority on what is so great
about the Gateway City. We provide our readers—both monthly through our
printed publications, and daily through our website—with useful, current
information that helps them make the most out of living in St. Louis. Through
our pages, St. Louisans can connect with their city in a whole new way.

Food Photography and Styling by Greg Rannells
Portrait Photography by Kevin A. Roberts

This book was produced by SLM Media Group.
1600 S. Brentwood, Ste. 550
St. Louis, MO 63144
314-918-3000 | stlmag.com

For Distribution Information call 314-918-3006.

A portion of the proceeds from the sale of this cookbook
is going to the support of Operation Food Search, the St. Louis region's
the largest distributor of free food for the hungry.

OPERATION
FOOD
SEARCH

INTRODUCTION

Over the past decade, St. Louis' culinary scene has exploded with vibrant young chefs, new restaurants, and new dishes at the old standbys. While for years, no one could fault the city in terms of Italian food and slab of steak, today St. Louis can go toe to toe with just every metropolitan area in terms of fabulous food being served in our dining establishments.

So, with that development in mind, we decided to create this cookbook by asking all of the area's top chefs to send in recipes, as well as reprinting recipes that have shown up over the past eight years in the pages of *St. Louis* AT HOME. With every cookbook purchased, we are proud to report that a portion will be donated to an outstanding organization, Operation Food Search.

The chefs chosen include many we have featured over the years in the pages of *St. Louis Magazine*. The reaction was impressive. Herewith you have more than 170 recipes, great dishes served at restaurants that you can now recreate at home—and the equivalent of several months worth of meal planning. We have a smattering of offerings from some of the state's top talent, but the bulk of this book comes from chefs working everywhere from downtown to Wildwood.

This cookbook differs from other chef-driven cookbooks in two ways: We specifically asked chefs for recipes that could be prepared "by the average cook with a typically-equipped kitchen and pantry," i.e., nothing too exotic or overwrought. We know you wouldn't attempt those anyway.

In addition, we asked for a broad range of recipes, items not just from the chefs' respective restaurants, but their favorite recipes—items they created but never used in their restaurants, items passed down through generations of their families, even items they make only for their own family.

St. Louis is a great restaurant town. We hope we've brought a little of that home.

Enjoy,

Christy   *Mahe*

Christy Marshall, Editor-in-Chief, *St. Louis* AT HOME and *St. Louis Family*
George Mahe, Dining Editor, *St. Louis Magazine*

CONTENTS

RECIPES FROM ST. LOUIS' AND MISSOURI'S TOP CHEFS

Appetizers

SMOKED SALMON CANAPÉS

TONY ALMOND, ALMONDS RESTAURANT

SERVES 6

2 cups whipped cream cheese

2 tablespoons capers, chopped

2 tablespoons green onions, chopped

Juice and zest of 1 lemon

Pinch kosher salt

Toast points, your choice of bread

1 pound smoked salmon

Black olives, sliced (optional)

Tomato, diced (optional)

Combine the cream cheese, capers, green onions, lemon juice, and lemon zest. Add the salt and mix thoroughly. Spread the desired amount on the toast points. Top with whole-flake pieces of smoked salmon.

Garnish with slices of black olive and cubes of chopped tomato, if desired. Serve chilled.

CRAWFISH HUSH PUPPIES WITH RÉMOULADE SAUCE

KELLY ENGLISH, KELLY ENGLISH STEAKHOUSE

SERVES 4

1 cup all-purpose flour

2 cups cornmeal

2 tablespoons baking powder

1 tablespoon kosher salt

¼ cup white sugar

1 tablespoon red pepper flakes

2 eggs

1¼ cups milk

1 cup corn kernels

1 cup crawfish tail meat*

1 tablespoon chopped tarragon

Canola oil

Remoulade sauce (recipe follows)

Separately mix together all of the dry ingredients and the eggs, milk, and corn kernels. Combine the dry and wet mixtures, being careful not to overwork. Stir in the crawfish and tarragon. Heat the canola oil in a cast-iron skillet over medium-high heat, and fry tablespoon-sized dollops of the batter until golden brown. Serve with remoulade sauce.

The crawfish can be replaced with almost anything: diced Andouille sausage, crabmeat, whatever you like.

REMOULADE SAUCE

1¼ cups mayonnaise

1 cup creole mustard

½ cup prepared horseradish

Juice of 1 lemon

¼ cup white wine vinegar

1 teaspoon granulated garlic

2 teaspoons onion powder

1 tablespoon celery salt

2 teaspoons snipped fresh chives

½ tablespoon kosher salt

1 teaspoon granulated sugar

Combine all of the ingredients and mix thoroughly.

TRUFFLE BUTTER POPCORN

MARC FELIX, CONSULTING CHEF

SERVES 2 TO 4

¼ cup black jewel popcorn

1 tablespoon black truffle butter, melted

1 teaspoon black truffle oil

½ teaspoon black truffle salt

Pop the popcorn in a hot-air popper. Drizzle the melted truffle butter over the popped corn, tossing to coat. (This works well with two people.) Follow with truffle oil and truffle salt, gently tossing to coat well. *Ingredients can be found at igourmet.com*

BREADED ARTICHOKES WITH LEMON AÏOLI

DOMINIC GALATI, DOMINIC'S ON THE HILL, DOMINIC'S TRATTORIA, AND GIO'S RISTORANTE & BAR

SERVES 6

3 eggs, lightly beaten

1 cup half-and-half

3 cups breadcrumbs

1 cup Parmesan cheese

½ cup chopped parsley

1 teaspoon crushed red pepper

Salt and pepper, to taste

2 16-ounce cans marinated artichoke hearts

1 cup all-purpose flour

Canola oil

Lemon aïoli (recipe follows)

Combine the eggs and the half-and-half, whisking until the eggs are lightly beaten. In a separate bowl, combine the breadcrumbs, Parmesan, parsley, crushed red pepper, salt, and pepper. Mix well. Drain the artichokes and cut each in half.

Toss each artichoke in the flour, shaking off any excess. Dip each artichoke into the egg wash, then toss in the breadcrumbs. Coat a cast-iron skillet with canola oil and heat until very hot. Pan-fry the breaded artichokes until golden brown and crispy. Serve with lemon aïoli.

LEMON AÏOLI

3 large egg yolks

1 cup olive oil (or vegetable oil of your choice)

1 teaspoon lemon juice

½ teaspoon cold water

½ teaspoon chopped garlic

Combine all of the ingredients in a blender, and blend until thick.

CRUDO

REX HALE, THREE SIXTY

SERVES 4

2 cups arugula

8 ounces sashimi-grade walu or Hawaiian escolar, thinly sliced

8 ounces sashimi-grade tuna, thinly sliced

2 limes, peel and pith removed, quartered

1 ripe, firm avocado, thinly sliced

Flor de Sal* and freshly ground black pepper, to taste

4 tablespoons high-quality extra-virgin olive oil

Assorted micro basil, chiffonade

Divide the arugula between four plates and arrange alternating slices of walu and tuna over the top. Garnish with lime wedges and slices of avocado. Season to taste with Flor de Sal and freshly ground black pepper, then squeeze ¼ lime over each plate. Drizzle with extra-virgin olive oil and sprinkle the micro basil.

Available at amazon.com.

BARBECUE OYSTERS

REX HALE, THREE SIXTY

SERVES 4

3 tablespoons minced garlic

1 large shallot, minced

½ teaspoon red pepper flakes

1 teaspoon smoked sea salt

½ red bell pepper, minced

½ cup extra-virgin olive oil

8 ounces (2 sticks) unsalted butter

1 small bunch parsley, finely chopped

16 large oysters (Blue Point or similar) on the half-shell

2 lemons, peel, pith, and seeds removed, cut into wedges

Preheat the oven to 500 degrees. Lightly sauté the garlic, shallots, red pepper flakes, salt, and bell pepper in the olive oil, then cool slightly. Meanwhile, whip the butter in an electric mixer until it doubles in volume. With the mixer on low speed, add the vegetable mixture and then add the parsley.

Arrange the oysters in a single layer in an ovenproof baking dish. Spoon the butter mixture over the oysters and bake until browned slightly. Serve on sea salt-lined plates and garnish with lemon wedges.

MEATBALL SLIDERS

REX HALE, THREE SIXTY

SERVES 4

1 pound grass-fed ground beef

1 tablespoon garlic, minced

1 tablespoon yellow onion, minced

1 large egg

1 tablespoon coarse sea salt

1 teaspoon freshly ground black pepper

2 tablespoons parsley, chopped

½ cup good Parmesan cheese, grated

2 tablespoons dry breadcrumbs

1 cup pomodoro sauce (recipe follows)

¾ cup shredded provolone cheese

12 good-quality store-bought slider buns

½ cup chiffonade of fresh basil mixed with 2 to 3 tablespoons grated Parmesan

Preheat the oven to 400 degrees.

Combine the ground beef with the next eight ingredients and chill for about an hour. Scoop and shape into twelve 1½-ounce balls. Bake for about 20 minutes, then top each meatball with 1 tablespoon pomodoro sauce and provolone. Return to the oven until the cheese is melted. Place 1 tablespoon sauce on each half of the slider buns, top with a meatball and a sprinkling of the basil-Parmesan mixture.

POMODORO SAUCE

1 large yellow onion, finely diced

½ cup extra-virgin olive oil

3 teaspoons garlic, minced

2 cups tomato paste

½ cup white wine

¼ cup sugar

3 pounds roma tomatoes, chopped

3 cups water

Salt and fresh black pepper, to taste

1 small bunch fresh parsley, finely chopped

2 ounces fresh basil, finely chopped

2 tablespoons fresh oregano, finely chopped

1 tablespoon fresh thyme, finely chopped

In a large stockpot, sweat the onions in the olive oil until translucent; add the garlic, tomato paste, white wine, and sugar, and stir to combine. Add the roma tomatoes and water, then simmer for about an hour. Using an immersion blender (or a food processor, working in batches), purée the sauce and season to taste with salt and pepper. Remove from heat and add all the fresh herbs. Taste and adjust seasoning as needed.

ARANCINI DI ROSA GABRIELE (FRIED RICE BALLS)

PAUL GABRIELE, AGOSTINO'S

SERVES 4

1 ½ cups arborio rice

8 ounces ground beef

½ cup green peas, precooked and salted

½ cup mozzarella cheese, cubed or diced

1 ounce prosciutto ham, diced

3 eggs, separated

2 cups Italian bread crumbs

2 teaspoons olive oil

¼ cup butter

1 ounce Parmesan cheese

1 ounce yellow onion

¼ cup white wine

¼ cup tomato paste

½ teaspoon saffron

RICE PREPARATION

In a medium-size pot, lightly brown the chopped onion in butter and olive oil. Over medium heat, add rice. Stir in a cup of water at a time and stir constantly until 3 cups of water is absorbed. The rice should cook for at least 15 minutes or until al dente. Remove the rice from heat and spread the rice out in a large flat rimmed pan. Cool for 20 minutes. Add Parmesan cheese and one egg yolk. Stir until completely blended. Season with salt and pepper to taste.

BEEF MIXTURE PREPARATION

In a separate saucepan, place 1 ounce of butter and 7 ounces of ground beef. Over medium heat, cook the beef until browned. Add wine, salt, and pepper to taste. Then add tomato paste and stir until dissolved. When beef mix has cooked, place ground beef in a large flat rimmed pan, spread the beef mix out, and allow to cool for 20 minutes. Add prosciutto, mozzarella cheese, and green peas. It is very important that this mixture is dry.

FOR THE RICE BALLS/ARANCINI

Place a tablespoon or so of rice mixture into the palm of your hand and press the rice against the palm until almost flat. In the center of the palmed rice mix, add a ball of the ground beef mixture (1 teaspoon or so) and cover with a little more rice mixture to form a baseball-like shape and size. Roll the rice mixture into a ball form with both hands. Continue until all the rice mixture is used up. Generally, smaller rice balls are better.

Season the bread-crumb mix with a pinch of salt and pepper. Place the rice balls in a bowl of beaten egg whites only. Coat the entire rice ball with the egg white batter and then roll the rice ball directly into the breadcrumbs until completely covered.

Place rice balls in a deep fryer with vegetable oil at 350 degrees until toasted golden brown or not more than five minutes. Serve hot. Garnish with sprig of parsley.

OVEN-ROASTED ARTICHOKE WITH CREAM OF BRIE AND WHOLE-GRAIN MUSTARD BUTTER SAUCE

ERIC KELLY, SCAPE AMERICAN BISTRO

SERVES 4

4 large artichokes

12 ounces cream of Brie cheese

Whole grain mustard-butter sauce (recipe follows)

Bring a large stockpot of salted water to a boil. Meanwhile, trim the stems and ½ inch off the top of the artichokes. Add the trimmed artichokes to the boiling water, covering the pot with a plate to completely submerge them. Boil for exactly 25 minutes. Remove the artichokes from the water and submerge them into a large bowl of ice water. Let cool completely, then drain them upside down for 15 minutes. Reach into the center of each artichoke and, using your fingers, pull out all of the thistle and fuzz and discard.

Preheat the oven to 400 degrees.

Smear equal amounts of cheese under the petals and in the center of the artichokes. Bake for 10 to 12 minutes, then remove to serving plates. Drizzle the sauce over the top and around each artichoke. Serve.

WHOLE-GRAIN MUSTARD BUTTER SAUCE

1 teaspoon extra-virgin olive oil

1 tablespoon minced shallots

¼ cup white wine

¼ cup rice wine vinegar

1 tablespoon heavy cream

Pinch kosher salt

Pinch fresh-cracked white pepper

8 ounces (2 sticks) butter, chilled and cut into ½-inch dice

1 tablespoon whole-grain mustard

Heat the olive oil in a stainless steel sauté pan over medium heat. Add the shallots and sweat for 4 to 5 minutes or until translucent; do not brown shallots the least bit. Add the wine and vinegar and reduce until nearly dry. Add the cream and reduce by half. Add the butter all at once and constantly whisk until 95 percent of the butter is melted. Remove from the heat and continue whisking until the butter is completely melted. Strain the sauce into a pan and discard the shallots. Keep in a warm area of the kitchen until ready to serve.

SHRIMP & SCALLOP CEVICHE

ERIC KELLY, SCAPE AMERICAN BISTRO

SERVES 4

16 8-inch corn tortillas

Vegetable oil for frying

1 shrimp and scallop ceviche (recipe follows)

4 tablespoons red bell pepper, ¼-inch dice

4 tablespoons yellow bell pepper, ¼-inch dice

4 tablespoons celery, ¼-inch dice

4 tablespoons red onion, ¼-inch dice

1 avocado, ½-inch dice

2 tablespoons chopped cilantro, plus 4 cilantro sprigs

Kosher salt, to taste

Fresh-cracked black pepper, to taste

¼ cup extra-virgin olive oil

4 lime wedges

Stack the tortillas, eight in a pile, and cut like a pizza into sixths. Deep fry the wedges in vegetable oil until crispy. Drain on paper towels and let cool. Drain off half of the citrus juice from the ceviche and discard. Place the peppers, celery, red onion, avocado, and chopped cilantro into a mixing bowl. Season to taste with salt and pepper and stir to combine evenly. Add the vegetable mixture to the ceviche. Drizzle the olive oil over the mixture and toss to emulsify.

Divide the mixture between four serving bowls. Garnish with a lime wedge and a cilantro sprig. Serve with the corn tortilla chips.

SHRIMP AND SCALLOP CEVICHE

- 1 cup fresh lime juice
- ½ cup fresh lemon juice
- 20 large raw shrimp (26/30 count), tail off
- 8 large raw scallops (10 count)

Combine both juices in a nonreactive mixing bowl or plastic container. Cut the shrimp in half lengthwise and quarter the scallops. Place the seafood in the citrus juice mixture and stir to combine evenly. Cover and refrigerate overnight.

BUFFALO-STYLE OYSTERS

NICK MILLER, HARVEST

SERVES 4

The freshness of the oyster plays a crucial role in the success of the dish—a fresh oyster will smell like an ocean breeze. Oysters may range from 1½ inches to 3½ inches in length. The smaller oyster will pack a flavorful punch and should not be overlooked simply because of its size. The origin of the oyster also plays a huge role in its bouquet and flavor profiles.

Oenophiles use the term terroir to explain why wine will have certain subtle nuances; for oysters, it is the water they inhabit that will reveal itself to you through the flavor. For frying, I generally use a plump, medium oyster such as a Blue Point or Sunset Beach.

- ½ cup rice flour
- 1 tablespoon cornstarch
- ½ teaspoon salt
- 3 ounces club soda
- ¼ cup hot sauce
- ¼ teaspoon lime juice
- 1 teaspoon honey
- ½ teaspoon salt
- 1 teaspoon Dijon mustard
- 1 tablespoon unsalted butter
- 1 tablespoon blue cheese (I prefer an acidic blue like Maytag or Point Reyes)
- 2 tablespoons buttermilk
- 3 tablespoons mayonnaise
- ¼ teaspoon lemon juice
- ¼ teaspoon red onion, minced
- Salt and pepper, to taste
- 12 oysters on the half shell
- Vegetable oil for frying
- Finely chopped celery

Make the tempura batter: Combine the rice flour, cornstarch and salt, then add the club soda and whisk together into a loose paste. Reserve and keep chilled.

In a saucepan over medium heat, stir together the hot sauce, lime juice, honey, salt, and Dijon mustard, and bring to a simmer. Whisk in the butter, then remove from the heat and reserve.

Mash the blue cheese into the buttermilk with a fork. Whisk in the mayonnaise, lemon juice, red onion, salt, and pepper.

CONTINUED ON PG. 18

Wood-Grilled Flatbread with Zephyr Squash, Fresh Ricotta, and Honey

CARY McDOWELL, WINSLOW'S HOME

SERVES 4

Extra-virgin olive oil

2 prebaked pizza shells*

8 ounces ricotta cheese
(the dryer, the better)

Salt

Pepper

2 Zephyr or other fresh-
picked sweet summer
squashes

Thyme

Honey

Most home cooks don't have a wood-fired pizza oven, but a Weber Kettle charcoal grill will work just as well. Place a pizza stone on the grill over a hardwood fire, and get the fire as hot as possible, so it functions like a wood-fired pizza oven.

Preheat the grill and pizza stone or preheat the oven to 425 degrees

Drizzle olive oil on each pizza shell. Smear half of the ricotta on the shells and season to taste with salt and pepper.

Slice the squash lengthwise, paper-thin. Place the slices on the pizza shells and again drizzle with olive oil, salt, and pepper. Top with irregular spoonfuls of the remaining ricotta cheese, and season them with salt and pepper.

Put the pizzas in the oven or on the pizza stone on the grill. Assuming it's as hot as discussed earlier, bake the pizzas for 2 to 3 minutes, or until the edges are crispy. Remove from the heat.

Allow to cool for a minute, then cut the pizzas. Pull fresh thyme leaves off the stems and scatter over the pizzas. Crack fresh black pepper from a pepper mill on top, and drizzle with your favorite honey.

I recommend an artisanal flatbread or pizza dough, like those at Breadsmith, which have a good balance of crispness and chewiness.

** The pizza may be assembled up to 4 hours ahead and baked just before serving.*

Remove the oysters from the half shells and lightly coat them in the tempura batter. Drop them one at a time into a 350-degree fryer. Remove the oysters from the oil after approximately 1 minute. They should be a light golden color. Briefly drain them on paper towels. Transfer to the saucepan and lightly coat with the buffalo sauce.

Spoon the blue cheese mixture on to the half shells, then top each with a buffalo sauced oyster. Garnish with the celery.

THE DEVILED OYSTER WITH BACON CREAMED SPINACH

NICK MILLER, HARVEST

SERVES 4

3 ounces bacon, diced into ¼-inch squares

½ cup cream

2 inch sprig rosemary

2 sprigs thyme

4 cloves garlic, smashed

8 ounces spinach

Salt and pepper, to taste

12 oysters on the half shell

½ cup buttermilk

½ cup cornmeal

½ cup all-purpose flour

1 teaspoon cayenne pepper

1 teaspoon black pepper

Vegetable oil for frying

Place the bacon in a pan and cook over medium heat, stirring often. When thoroughly browned, remove from heat and drain on paper towels. Reserve. Add

the cream, herbs, and garlic to a saucepot. Place over medium-low heat and reduce by half. Strain the cream through a fine-mesh strainer, discard the solids, and reserve. Blanch the spinach by placing it in boiling water for 1 minute, then drain. Toss the bacon, cream mixture, and spinach in a sauté pan and season to taste with salt and pepper. Remove the oysters from the shells. Scrub the shells and set aside. Place the oysters in the buttermilk. Thoroughly mix together the cornmeal, flour, cayenne, and black pepper. Take the oysters out of the buttermilk and place them in the cornmeal mixture. Coat them completely and place them into a 350-degree fryer until the oysters are golden brown. Season with salt.

Divide the warm spinach mixture between the half shells and top each with a fried oyster.

CARAMELIZED SCALLOPS WITH CLEMENTINE, CAULIFLOWER PURÉE, AND CAPERS

AARON TEITELBAUM, HERBIE'S VINTAGE 72

SERVES 4

½ pound cauliflower, trimmed, head cut into 1-inch florets, stem peeled and cut into ½-inch slices

Salt and freshly ground pepper, to taste

6 tablespoons unsalted butter, divided

2 tablespoons extra-virgin olive oil

1 tablespoon lemon juice

1 pound large dry-packed scallops

2 clementines, supremed

1 tablespoon capers, soaked in cold water for
20 minutes, rinsed and drained
1 tablespoon finely chopped Italian parsley

Bring a medium saucepan of salted water to a boil. Add the cauliflower to the pan and boil until the cauliflower pieces are tender when pierced with the tip of a paring knife, approximately 7 minutes. Remove from the heat and drain well.

Put the cooked cauliflower into the work bowl of a food processor and pulse until smooth. Season the cauliflower to taste with salt and pepper and add 2 tablespoons butter. Pulse to combine, taking care not to overwork the mixture. Transfer the purée to the top of a double boiler, and press a piece of plastic wrap directly against the surface of the purée.

Warm the remaining 4 tablespoons of butter and the olive oil in a large sauté pan over high heat. Pat the scallops dry, then season them with the lemon juice, salt, and pepper. Add the scallops and sear until lightly browned on one side; flip and sear the other side. Transfer the scallops to a warm plate.

[Editor's note: To supreme the clementines: Slice the peel and pith off the fruit with a sharp paring knife by following the contour of the fruit. Cut out the segments from between each membrane.]

Keep the pan over high heat and, when the butter turns light golden brown, add the clementines, capers, and parsley. Return the scallops to the pan, season to taste with salt and pepper and sauté just until warmed through, about 1 minute.

Divide the cauliflower purée between four warm soup plates or shallow bowls. Arrange the scallops atop the purée, then spoon some of the clementine sauce over the scallops.

MOREL PASTA WITH PORT WINE CREAM SAUCE

AARON TEITELBAUM, HERBIE'S VINTAGE 72

SERVES 6

1 pound morel mushrooms
2 tablespoons butter
1 750-ml bottle port wine
5 shallots, chopped
3 cloves garlic, chopped
2 quarts heavy whipping cream
½ cup cornstarch
½ cup water
1 pound linguini, cooked to al dente
Gruyère cheese
Fresh tarragon

Cut the mushrooms in half. Rinse them thoroughly, then submerge them in salted water and soak for 15 minutes. Drain, then submerge the mushrooms two to three times in fresh water.

Heat the butter in a large sauté pan. When the butter is bubbling, add the mushrooms and sauté for 3 to 5 minutes or until the mushrooms release their liquid. Season to taste with salt and pepper.

Combine the port wine, shallots, and garlic in a saucepan; bring to a simmer and reduce by ⅔. Add the heavy whipping cream and bring to boil. Whisk together the cornstarch and water, then add the slurry to the pan. Stir to combine, then simmer until thickened. Season to taste with salt and pepper.

Toss the cooked linguini with the sauce. Divide into individual pasta bowls, then top with the sautéed morels. Garnish with a sprinkle of grated Gruyère cheese and fresh tarragon.

BAJA SHRIMP COCKTAIL

JAMES VOSS, DUFF'S

SERVES 4

½ pound medium (41/50) shrimp in the shell

1 tablespoon canola oil

½ teaspoon Old Bay seasoning

¼ cup hot sauce plus ½ teaspoon, divided

¼ teaspoon kosher salt

¼ teaspoon black pepper

12 ounces of your favorite beer

1 cup fresh tomato, deseeded and diced

1 bunch fresh cilantro, chopped

1 bunch green onion, chopped

¼ cup red onion, chopped

Chopped jalapeños, to taste (or habaneros if desired)

1 or more diced avocado, as desired

¼ cup ketchup

2 tablespoons fresh-squeezed orange juice

2 tablespoons fresh-squeezed lime juice

In a medium sauce pan, sauté the shrimp in the canola oil over high heat for 30 seconds. Add the Old Bay seasoning, hot sauce, kosher salt, black pepper, and beer. Bring the mixture to a boil. Toss to cook evenly. Cook until the shrimp is just pink. Do not overcook. Drain, reserving the liquid. Place the shrimp in ice water to chill, then peel and chop the shrimp into large chunks.

In a bowl, combine shrimp with the tomato, fresh cilantro, green and red onions, jalapeños, and avocado.

In a separate bowl, whisk together ¼ cup of the reserved cooking liquid, the remaining ¼ cup hot sauce (or more, to taste), ketchup, and the orange and lime juices. Add the dressing to the shrimp mixture, toss well, and chill. Serve with tortilla chips.

BRUSCHETTA DI POMODORO

JAMES VOSS, DUFF'S

SERVES 4

2 cups high-quality tomatoes, deseeded and diced

¼ cup fresh basil, finely julienned

¼ cup olive oil

½ teaspoon kosher salt

½ teaspoon fresh-cracked black pepper

½ teaspoon minced fresh garlic

2 cups balsamic vinegar

1 baguette, cut into thick slices

8 ounces soft goat cheese

Parmigiano-Reggiano cheese

Place the tomatoes, basil, olive oil, salt, pepper, and garlic in a bowl and toss to combine thoroughly.

Place the balsamic vinegar in a small saucepan over medium-low heat and cook until the vinegar is reduced and measures ½ cup. (Do not over-reduce or it will turn bitter.) Let cool and refrigerate until just before ready to use.

Toast the baguette slices. Spread each slice with goat cheese, then top each with the tomato-basil mixture. Drizzle with balsamic syrup and shave Parmigiano-Reggiano over the top.

Breakfast, Brunch & Lunch

BOMBAY PANINI
STEVEN BECKER,
NADOZ EURO BAKERY & CAFÉ
SERVES 1

1 cup mayonnaise

2 teaspoons curry powder

1 tablespoon fresh lemon juice

Salt and white pepper, to taste

1 naan*

1 tablespoon fresh cilantro, chopped

2 slices pepper jack cheese

4 ounces grilled chicken breast

¼ cup fresh spinach leaves

Prepare the curry mayo by mixing the mayonnaise, curry powder, and lemon juice. Season with salt and pepper to taste.

Cut the naan in half. Spread ¼ cup of the curry mayo on both sides. Sprinkle the cilantro on one side of the naan bread and place the cheese slices on the other side.

Slice the grilled chicken breast lengthwise to fully fit across ½ the bread. Top with the spinach. Assemble the sandwich and grill on a panini press for 5 minutes or until hot throughout. (Alternately, if you don't have a panini press, use a nonstick skillet and cook the panini as you would a grilled cheese sandwich, buttering the bread and weighting the sandwich with another heavy skillet.)

*Nadoz bakes naan in-house, which can be purchased if preordered. Naan is also available at Costco and at specialty grocers.

LOBSTER ROLLS
BRIAN S. HALE
SERVES 8

½ cup mayonnaise

1 tablespoon chopped fresh tarragon

1 teaspoon lemon zest

2 tablespoons fresh lemon juice

1 pound cooked lobster claw meat

Kosher salt, to taste

Black pepper, to taste

8 small brioche rolls

1 lemon, cut into wedges

Mix the mayonnaise, tarragon, zest, and juice together and reserve. In a large bowl, combine the lobster claw meat with the mayonnaise mixture, being careful not to break up the lobster too much. Season to taste with salt and pepper. Toast the buns and divide the lobster filling between them. Serve with a lemon wedge.

MY FAVORITE STEAK SANDWICH
DANA HOLLAND,
JILLY'S CUPCAKE BAR & CAFÉ
SERVES 2

This is a dish I love to serve in my restaurants and make for myself. It is a beef-lover's dish without the pomp. And it's easy to make for two, because one steak will feed both of you.

1 10- to 14-ounce New York strip steak

1 tablespoon vegetable oil

1 teaspoon whole black peppercorns

½ teaspoon fennel seed

½ teaspoon coriander seed

2 teaspoons kosher or sea salt

1 tablespoon chopped fresh rosemary

2 thick slices ciabatta bread

6 tablespoons olive oil

2 cloves garlic, sliced thinly

3 cups spinach, arugula or chard (pick one or use a mixture)

Pinch kosher or sea salt

Pinch ground black pepper or red pepper flakes

½ lemon

Pecorino-Romano or Parmigiano-Reggiano

Trim the steak of excess fat and rub it with vegetable oil. Using a spice grinder, coarsely grind the peppercorns, fennel seed, and coriander seed and mix with the salt and fresh rosemary. Rub on both sides of the steak and set aside until ready to cook. (You may do this up to 3 hours before cooking the steak. In any case, bring the steak to room temperature before cooking it.)

When ready to eat, heat a heavy-bottomed or cast-iron skillet. Add 1 tablespoon of olive oil and grill the bread on one side. Add another 1 tablespoon of olive oil and grill the other side. When golden, remove to a plate.

Reheat the skillet to very hot and add 1 tablespoon of olive oil. Add the steak and cook to your liking, about 6½ minutes total for rare. When done, remove to a clean plate and let rest.

Heat 1 tablespoon of olive oil in the skillet and add the garlic. Toast until golden, about 1 minute, and then add the mixed greens. Add a pinch of salt and a pinch of pepper or red pepper flakes and toss once or twice until wilted.

To serve, set a slice of ciabatta on each plate. Slice the steak on the bias and divide among the two plates.

Drizzle over any accumulated juices. Divide the greens over the top of the steak. Squeeze a little lemon juice over each steak and drizzle each steak with 1 tablespoon of olive oil. Top with more pepper or red pepper flakes for a bolder flavor, and finish with a few shavings of Parmigiano-Reggiano.

SALMON BLT

ALI IGLESIAS, THE BOATHOUSE

SERVES 1

1 cup mayonnaise

1 teaspoon lemon juice

2 ounces fresh basil, chopped

2 cups apple cider vinegar

¼ cup brown sugar

1 teaspoon Spanish paprika

1 teaspoon yellow mustard

1 teaspoon salt

1 teaspoon ground black pepper

1 4- to 6-ounce salmon filet

2 slices sourdough bread

4 strips applewood-smoked bacon, cooked

Red leaf lettuce, washed

2 tomatoes, sliced

Combine the mayonnaise, lemon juice and basil in a large bowl, mixing well until incorporated. Refrigerate until ready to use.

Combine the cider vinegar, brown sugar, paprika, mustard, salt, and pepper in a large bowl, mixing well. Add the salmon filet and marinate for about 2 hours. Keep refrigerated until ready to use.

Preheat oven to 400 degrees. Place the marinated salmon on a sheet pan and bake for approximately 8 to 10 minutes. Place the bread slices on a sheet pan and

**DAVID KIRKLAND,
CAFÉ OSAGE**

Your favorite Sunday dinner? Anything cooked by my wife.

Your favorite kitchen tool? Zester.

The one ingredient kitchen pantries should always have? Paprika.

What dish do your children ask you to make? Enchiladas.

What is your favorite restaurant (aside from your own)? Farmhaus.

BrieLT

DAVID KIRKLAND, CAFÉ OSAGE

SERVES 4

4 tablespoons tomato
jam (recipe follows)

4 slices whole-wheat
bread, toasted

16 slices bacon, cooked

12 thin slices Brie cheese

1 cup arugula

The BrieLT has been the most popular item on the menu at Café Osage since its opening in August 2008. How can you go wrong with Brie and bacon? People are always asking for the tomato jam recipe so they can make this sandwich at home.

Spread 1 tablespoon of tomato jam on each slice of the toasted bread. Top each slice with four slices of bacon and three slices of brie cheese. Place under the broiler until the cheese is melted. Top with a handful of arugula. Cut each open-faced sandwich into half.

TOMATO JAM (MAKES 1 QUART)

2 tablespoons olive oil

1 white onion, diced

1 tablespoon dry mustard

1 tablespoon cinnamon

1 tablespoon allspice

2 cups sugar

12 cups fresh or canned diced tomatoes (If
you use canned, use the juice too.)

2 cups apple cider vinegar

In a 4-quart pot, heat the olive oil. Add the onion and sweat them until translucent and soft. Add the dry mustard, cinnamon, allspice, and sugar and cook until the sugar has melted, stirring continually to prevent the mixture from sticking. Add the tomatoes and vinegar. Cook over low heat for about 2 hours, until the mixture is thick and the consistency of jam, stirring occasionally to prevent sticking and burning.

Veggie Hash

MIKE RANDOLPH, HALF & HALF

SERVES 2

1 tablespoon butter

1 cup Brussels sprouts, cleaned and blanched

½ onion, diced and caramelized

½ cup potato, cubed and roasted

2 cups baby spinach

Salt and pepper, to taste

2 eggs, sunny side up

Heat a cast-iron skillet over medium heat, add the butter and the Brussels sprouts and sauté until the sprouts are lightly browned. Add the onion, potato, and spinach and season to taste with salt and pepper. Once the spinach has wilted down, top with the sunny side up eggs and serve.

Soups
&Salads

COMPANION'S FAMOUS TOMATO BISQUE

JODI ALLEN,
COMPANION BAKERY & CAFÉ

SERVES 10 TO 12

2 shallots

¼ cup garlic paste*

1 tablespoon olive oil

¼ bottle dry white wine

1 28-ounce can crushed tomatoes

1 28-ounce can tomato sauce

8 cups water

½ cup vegetable base*

1 stick butter

¾ cup plus 2 tablespoons flour

4 cups whole milk

1 cup 40-percent cream

Fresh basil, shredded

In a food processor, mince the shallots with the garlic paste.

In a large stockpot, heat the oil. Add the shallot mixture and sauté until the bottom of the pot is brown. Deglaze the pot with the wine; bring to a simmer and reduce for 5 to 10 minutes. Add the tomatoes, tomato sauce, water, and vegetable base. Cover the pot, and bring to a boil.

In a separate small pot, melt butter. Add the flour and stir to combine. Cook the roux to a light blonde color. Add the roux to the boiling pot and whisk vigorously. Add the milk and cream, and stir to combine. Cook until warmed through.

Portion into serving bowls, and top with shredded fresh basil.

Find garlic paste and vegetable base at the grocery store, usually in the same section as spices or boullion.

ROASTED BUTTERNUT SQUASH SOUP

JODI ALLEN,
COMPANION BAKERY & CAFÉ

SERVES 8

4 pounds butternut squash, peeled, seeded, and diced

2 yellow onions, diced

2 apples, peeled, cored, and diced

3 tablespoons olive oil

¾ teaspoon kosher salt

¾ teaspoon ground black pepper

3 cups chicken stock

½ teaspoon curry powder

1 green onion, chopped

Preheat the oven to 425 degrees. Place the squash, onions, and apples on a sheet pan, and toss with the olive oil, salt, and pepper. Roast for 30 to 40 minutes or until very tender.

Meanwhile, heat the chicken stock until it is simmering. When the vegetables are done, purée them in batches in a food processor and transfer to a large pot. (You can add some additional chicken stock into the processor to puree with the veggies, if necessary.) Add enough of the warm chicken stock to the pot to make a thick soup. Add the curry powder, stir to combine and cook over medium heat until heated through. Stir in the green onion just before serving.

TWO-BEAN SOUP

JODI ALLEN,
COMPANION BAKERY & CAFÉ

SERVES 10 TO 12

4 tablespoons olive oil

1 ½ cups onion, diced

¾ cup carrots, diced

¾ cup celery, diced

1 teaspoon kosher salt

3 garlic cloves, minced

5 cups vegetable stock, divided

8 cups kale, chopped

2 15-ounce cans white beans, drained

2 15-ounce cans black beans, drained

Pepper, to taste

1 ½ tablespoons red wine vinegar

1 ½ teaspoons fresh rosemary, chopped

In a large stockpot, heat the olive oil. Add the onions, carrots, and celery and sauté until tender. Stir in the salt and garlic and cook for 1 minute. Add the kale and half of the vegetable stock and bring to a boil. Cover, reduce the heat and simmer for 3 minutes. Add the white and black beans, pepper, and the remaining vegetable stock; bring to a boil. Reduce the heat and add the vinegar and rosemary.

CHILLED AVOCADO, SPINACH, AND SORREL SOUP

BRAD BERACHA, ARAKA

SERVES 4

1 leek, medium dice

2 shallots, julienned

4 cloves garlic, sliced

1 pint white wine

1 pound fresh spinach

3 ½ cups vegetable stock, cold

½ cup heavy cream, cold

1 avocado

1 lemon, juiced

1 bunch Italian parsley (rough chop)

½ bunch sorrel

Sweat leek, shallot, and garlic. Deglaze the pan with the white wine. Reduce by half. Add spinach and cook until wilted. Add remaining ingredients and purée.

Chill and garnish with herbed crème fraiche, leek sautéed until crispy, and chiffonade of sorrel.

NEW ENGLAND FISH CHOWDER

BILL CARDWELL, CARDWELL'S AT THE
PLAZA AND BC'S KITCHEN

SERVES 10 TO 12

¼ pound salt pork, diced fine

4 tablespoons butter

2 onions, diced

2 bay leaves

1 tablespoon fresh thyme, minced

12 red new potatoes, large dice

1 ½ quarts fresh fish stock (recipe follows)

4 pounds fresh, firm fish (halibut, cod, hake), skinned and boneless, cut into 2-inch cubes

2 cups heavy cream

Salt and pepper, to taste

Parsley, minced

CONTINUED ON PG. 42

**STEVE KOMOREK,
TRATTORIA
MARCELLA**

Who taught you to cook?
Self taught. At 37, I went to a
slow-food program in Italy
and received my master's in
Italian food.

**Your favorite comfort
food?** Pizza.

**Your favorite restaurant in
town?** I'd say Brasserie.

**Your favorite kitchen
tool?** My pasta extruder
machine.

Cantaloupe Soup

STEVE KOMOREK, TRATTORIA MARCELLA

SERVES 8

5 slices prosciutto

2 medium-sized cantaloupes, seeded, peeled, and cubed

1 tablespoon honey

½ cup 40-percent heavy cream

1 lime, juiced

Pinch salt

Few twists of fresh-cracked pepper

½ cup golden raisins, steeped in Amaretto

½ cup crumbled Gorgonzola cheese

¼ cup parsley, chopped

Fry the prosciutto until crispy, then drain on paper towels. When cool enough to handle, crumble into pieces and reserve.

In a blender or food processor, purée the cubed cantaloupe. Add the honey, cream, lime juice, salt, and pepper and blend to combine.

Divide the soup into chilled cups, then top each with Gorgonzola crumbles, raisins, crispy prosciutto, and parsley.

2 bay leaves

4 leaves fresh sage

1 tablespoon chopped garlic

2 tablespoons plus oil

Salt and pepper

2 cups all-purpose flour

2 large eggs

Take 1 tablespoon of the oil and lightly coat the whole chicken. Season with salt and pepper and place in a preheated 375 degree oven. Roast for approximately 1 hour, or until the internal temperature reaches 165 degrees. When the chicken is done roasting, let rest until it is cool enough to handle with bare hands. You want to separate the meat from the bones, but do not throw anything away. Keep all bones, skin, cartilage, etc. separate from the meat. Start to pull all of the meat off the chicken and shred into small bite-size pieces, being careful not to include any bones in the meat. Keep all of the shredded meat separate.

Place a 1-gallon stockpot over medium heat. Add the other tablespoon of oil, 1½ cups of carrots, onion, celery thyme, bay leaves, sage, and garlic. Sauté until the vegetables start to sweat. Add the bones, skin, cartilage, and water to the pot. Bring to a low simmer, adjusting heat if necessary, and cook for approximately 3 hours.

Carefully strain the stock, and reserve the liquid, discarding the bones and vegetables.

EGG NOODLES

In a bowl, combine flour and a pinch of salt. Then make a well in the center. Add the eggs into the well, then gradually mix the flour into the egg, working from the inside out. Once you have formed a ball of dough, check the texture. If it is too sticky, add a bit more flour. If it is too dry, you can add a few drops of water. Remove the dough and lightly wrap in plastic. Let the dough rest for about 20 minutes.

On a well-floured surface, roll the dough out to about ⅛ inch thick. Let it air dry between 30 to 60 minutes. Flip the dough sheet over and let the other side dry between 30 to 60 minutes. Cut the dough into strips about ¼ inch wide and 3 inches long.

Place a gallon stockpot over medium heat. Add the chicken stock and pulled chicken meat, and bring to a simmer. Add the noodles and the remaining cup of diced carrots. Simmer for 10 to 12 minutes or until noodles are al dente. Stir every couple minutes so that noodles do not stick to the bottom of the pot. Season with salt and pepper to taste, and garnish with chopped parsley if desired.

SPINACH SALAD

TONY ALMOND,
ALMONDS RESTAURANT

SERVES 6

8 cups fresh baby spinach leaves

Crumbled feta cheese

1 red onion, thinly sliced

1 can mandarin oranges, drained

2 cups balsamic vinegar (use balsamic aged
   at least 9 years)

4 cloves garlic, peeled

Kosher salt, to taste

White pepper, to taste

Canola oil

Combine the spinach, feta, red onion, and mandarin oranges in a bowl.

Place the balsamic vinegar, garlic, salt, and pepper in a food processor and purée. With the motor running, add the canola oil in a thin stream until the mixture emulsifies and reaches the desired consistency.

Dress the salad with the desired amount of dressing and toss to combine.

SIMPLE MIXED GREENS SALAD

JIM FIALA, THE CROSSING, LILUMA,
LILUMA'S SIDE DOOR, AND ACERO

SERVES 8 TO 12

Monini olive oil*

Fresh lemon juice, strained, with zero pulp

2 pounds Granny Smith apples

2 pounds organic mixed greens

2 cups honey

3 tablespoons white truffle oil

Make the dressing by combining three parts olive oil to one part lemon juice, whisking until emulsified. The key is in the ratio; you should be able to taste both products, and the end product should have enough acidity to be slightly sour.

Core and julienne the apples into long matchsticks. Set aside. Wash the salad greens and set aside.

Pour the honey into a stainless-steel bowl. Slowly add the truffle oil, whisking until the oil is well-incorporated.

Gently toss the greens with the desired amount of dressing and apple matchsticks and divide onto serving plates. Finish by drizzling the desired amount of the honey mixture over the top.

Available at amazon.com

ARUGULA SALAD

REX HALE, THREE SIXTY

SERVES 4

5 ounces baby arugula

5 ounces watercress

4 ounces toasted whole walnuts or Missouri pecans

2 ounces fresh strawberries, thinly sliced

Honey vinaigrette (recipe follows)

2 ounces Baetje Farms fresh goat cheese

2 ounces dried strawberries (recipe below)

In a mixing bowl, toss together the arugula, watercress, nuts, and fresh strawberries. Add the desired amount of honey vinaigrette and toss to coat.

Arrange on four plates and garnish with goat cheese and dried strawberries.

DRIED STRAWBERRIES

1 cup warm water

1 cup sugar

Strawberries

Preheat the oven to 200 degrees.

Combine the water and sugar in a bowl.

Slice the strawberries thin, then dip them in the sugar water. Arrange the strawberries on a nonstick mat and bake for 45 minutes until dry.

HONEY VINAIGRETTE

1 tablespoon white balsamic vinegar

1 teaspoon honey

1 teaspoon Dijon mustard

1 teaspoon minced garlic

Salt and pepper to taste

¾ cup extra-virgin olive oil

CONTINUED ON PG. 48

JOSH GALLIANO

Your favorite comfort food when you go out? The whole fried catfish at Eagle's Nest in Addieville, IL.

Where do you go for pizza? The Good Pie.

One great cooking tip? Cook outside. ... Sear [your meat] outside with a cast iron skillet and a propane burner (like from your turkey fryer).

Which kitchen tool do you use the most? My hand blender.

German Potato Salad

JOSH GALLIANO

SERVES 8 TO 12

2 ½ pounds Yukon Gold potatoes

½ pound slab bacon

1 tablespoon canola oil

1 medium red onion, diced

4 tablespoons brown sugar

4 tablespoons red wine vinegar or cider vinegar

Water

4 hard-boiled eggs

Salt and pepper, to taste

Peel the potatoes and cut them into large dice. Store them in water until ready to use.

Chop the bacon, and render it in a large sauté pan with the canola oil. When the bacon begins to crisp, add the red onion. Sweat the onion until it is translucent, then add the brown sugar and vinegar to the pan. Stir to combine. Add the diced potatoes. Pour in enough water to almost cover the potatoes.

Bring to a boil, then lower the heat to simmer and cook until the potatoes are tender, about 20 minutes. If the potatoes cook before the water turns into a syrup, remove them from the pan and continue reducing the liquid until it forms a syrup. Then return the potatoes to the pan and toss to coat them with the syrup.

Slice the eggs and add them to the potato salad. Season to taste with salt and pepper.

Place all of the ingredients except the olive oil in a blender. Turn on the blender, then slowly add the olive oil until emulsified.

ROASTED-BEET SALAD

JOSH ROLAND, SALT

SERVES 10 TO 12

2 pounds assorted baby beets

½ cup strawberries, sliced

½ cup red-wine vinegar

1 cup niçoise or Kalamata olives, pitted

1 cup extra-virgin olive oil

1 cup feta cheese, crumbled

4 tablespoons horseradish, freshly grated

Fresh oregano leaves

For the dressing, purée extra-virgin olive oil and olives in a blender until smooth. Stir and strain.

Wrap beets in foil and roast for 1 hour at 375 degrees. Macerate strawberry pieces in red-wine vinegar for 30 minutes. Remove beets from oven, remove skin, and cut into small cubes. Mix with strawberries. Plate each salad. Sprinkle feta on top. Drizzle with 1 to 2 tablespoons of dressing. Add 1 teaspoon grated horseradish to each. Garnish with a few oregano leaves. Serve promptly.

SHRIMP AND MELON SALAD

DANA HOLLAND,
JILLY'S CUPCAKE BAR & CAFÉ

SERVES 4

This is a favorite of mine, and it is perfect for St. Louis summer days. Don't be intimidated by the length of this recipe—it's simple enough, and you can break up the separate parts to different days. To use as an appetizer, cut the amounts in half and serve in a large martini glass or scooped out mini melon; leave out the lettuce.

SHRIMP

1 ½ pounds large (21/25) shell-on shrimp

2 tablespoons Creole seasoning

1 tablespoon salt (if the Creole seasoning is unsalted)

1 lemon, sliced

DRESSING

3 lemons, juiced

2 limes, juiced

2 cloves garlic, peeled and minced

2 tablespoons pickled ginger, shredded

1 tablespoon pickled ginger juice

2 tablespoons honey

½ cup olive oil

2 tablespoons fresh basil, chopped

2 tablespoons fresh mint, chopped

2 tablespoons fresh cilantro, chopped

1 teaspoon sambal or red pepper flakes

Kosher salt, to taste

4 cups melon, peeled, seeded and diced*

SALAD

- 2 heads butter lettuce
- 1 cup jicama, julienned
- 1 cup fresh fennel, julienned
- 1 cup English cucumber, julienned
- 4 lemon wedges
- 4 lime wedges

Combine 1 gallon of water with the Creole seasoning, additional salt (if needed), and the lemon. Bring to a boil, lower the heat, and simmer for 15 minutes. Turn off the heat, add the shrimp and allow to steep in the hot water until cooked through, approximately 4 minutes. Drain and run under cold water until cooled. Immediately peel the shrimp. Split them in half lengthwise and remove any remaining residue. Set aside.

Combine all of the ingredients for the dressing except the melon and mix well, using more or less sambal to suit your taste. Toss with the shrimp and then stir in the melon. Allow to marinate for 1 hour or up to overnight.

Remove 12 of the largest leaves from the lettuce and place on individual plates. Divide the shrimp mixture among the four plates and surround the mixture with equal amounts of the julienned veggies. Dress with the remaining dressing from the shrimp. Serve with a wedge of lemon and lime and grilled pita bread.

* I love this salad with different colored and textured melons. The more you serve, the easier this is. If you are only making this for a few, however, select the ripest, sweetest melon you can find.

BRUSSELS SPROUTS AND CARAMELIZED ONION SALAD

WES JOHNSON

SERVES 8 TO 12

- 8 cups Brussels sprouts
- 2 tablespoons canola oil
- 2 medium onions
- 2/3 cup plus 3 tablespoons extra-virgin olive oil, divided
- 4 tablespoons white-wine vinegar
- 1 tablespoon Dijon mustard
- 1 tablespoon honey
- Coarse salt and ground pepper, to taste

Preheat the oven to 450 degrees.

Cut the brussels sprouts into quarters and toss them with the canola oil. Arrange in a shallow baking pan, cut sides down and in a single layer, and roast—without turning—for 40 to 45 minutes or until the outer leaves are tender and dark brown. Remove them from the oven and allow to cool.

Meanwhile, peel the onions and cut them into ½-inch wedges. In a wide skillet, heat 3 tablespoons olive oil over medium-high heat until the oil is hot but not smoking. Add the onions and stir to coat with oil. Reduce the heat to medium-low and cook, stirring occasionally, for 30 to 45 minutes or until the onions are softened and brown. Remove from the heat, stir once more, and allow to cool.

Make the vinaigrette: In a small bowl, whisk together the remaining 2/3 cup olive oil, vinegar, mustard and honey. Season to taste with coarse salt and pepper.

Toss the brussels sprouts, onions, and vinaigrette together in a large bowl. Place in refrigerator. Serve chilled.

Local White Asparagus-Grape Salad with Sherry Vinegar Sabayon

LOU ROOK III, ANNIE GUNN'S

SERVES 4

16 white asparagus
  spears
3 quarts water
1 cup lemon juice
¼ cup kosher salt
¼ cup sugar
1 cup sherry wine
⅓ cup sherry vinegar
2 egg yolks
⅓ cup extra virgin
  olive oil
Green and red grapes

Trim the ends of the asparagus about halfway up from the bottom. Gently peel the asparagus from the end of the tip to the bottom, being careful to not remove too much meat.

In a 4-quart stockpot, bring 3 quarts of water and 1 cup of lemon juice to a boil. Add the salt and sugar and resume the boil. Add the asparagus and cook about 4 minutes or until tender. Drain, then shock in ice water and drain again.

Place the sherry wine and vinegar in a small saucepan and simmer over medium heat. Reduce by ¾, cool and transfer to the top of double boiler. Add the yolks and set over simmering water on medium heat. Whisking constantly, cook until the yolks develop into thin ribbons. Remove from the heat and whisk in the extra virgin olive oil. If necessary, thin the sabayon with water or sherry vinegar and season to taste with salt and pepper.

Place the cooked asparagus on a serving platter and top with the desired amount of sabayon and grapes.

FRESH-CUT ARUGULA SALAD WITH CUCUMBERS, HEIRLOOM TOMATOES AND BUTTERMILK DRESSING

CARY McDOWELL, WINSLOW'S HOME

SERVES 4

4 large handfuls fresh-cut arugula

1 medium, fresh-picked cucumber

1 apple, cut into matchstick-size pieces

4 heirloom tomatoes (size and shape
 to taste)

4 tablespoons red-wine vinegar

1 egg yolk

¼ cup extra-virgin olive oil

¼ cup buttermilk

Salt and pepper

Wash the arugula by plunging it into ice-cold water, agitating firmly and letting it stand in the water for 1 minute. Transfer to a second bowl and repeat. Remove and spin dry. Store cold until ready to use.

Chop the cucumber and tomatoes into bite-sized pieces.

In a small mixing bowl, add a drop of water and the red-wine vinegar to the egg yolk. Whisk until the yolk becomes opaque in color, then slowly add the olive oil and whisk until the mixture is thick. Add the butter-milk and season to taste with salt and pepper.

Combine the arugula, cucumber, and tomatoes in a serving bowl. Add the desired amount of dressing and toss to combine. Serve immediately.

Make the vinaigrette: In a small bowl, whisk together the remaining ⅔ cup olive oil, vinegar, mustard, and honey. Season to taste with coarse salt and pepper. Set aside.

Wash the salad greens and set aside.

Pour the honey mixture into a stainless-steel bowl. Slowly add the truffle oil, whisking until the oil is well-incorporated.

Gently toss the greens with the desired amount of dressing and apple matchsticks and divide onto serving plates. Finish by drizzling the desired amount of the honey mixture over the top.

ORANGE-BRAISED BEET SALAD

CASSY VIRES, HOME WINE KITCHEN,

SERVES 4

1 ½ pounds beets, peeled, rinsed
 and quartered

3 tablespoons olive oil

¼ teaspoon salt

1 star anise

3 cinnamon sticks

1 head garlic, peeled

⅓ cup good-quality orange juice

Salt and pepper, to taste

4 ounces goat cheese, crumbled

4 handfuls arugula

¼ cup pine nuts, toasted

Preheat the oven to 375 degrees and line a roasting pan with aluminum foil. Combine the beets, oil, salt, anise, cinnamon sticks, garlic, and orange juice in the pan, tossing to coat the beets evenly. Spread the beets in a single layer and roast for about 45 minutes or until the beets are fork-tender. Refrigerate until cool. Discard the cinnamon stick and star anise pieces. Arrange the beet wedges on salad plates and season to taste with salt and pepper. Top with crumbled goat cheese, wild arugula, and pine nuts.

Entrées

Beef Wellington

WES JOHNSON
SERVES 8 TO 10

2 ½ pounds beef tenderloin, trimmed

Kosher salt and freshly ground black pepper, to taste

2 to 3 tablespoons olive oil

2 tablespoons whole-grain Dijon mustard

Flour, for dusting

1 pound puff pastry

2 eggs, lightly beaten

½ teaspoon coarse sea salt

Drizzle the beef with olive oil and season with the salt and black pepper. Heat a heavy skillet lightly coated with olive oil over medium-high heat. Reduce the heat to medium and sear the tenderloin on all sides, including the ends, for about 2 to 3 minutes total.

Remove the tenderloin to a plate and rub it lightly all over with the mustard. Allow to cool slightly then set it in the refrigerator for 30 minutes to ensure the tenderloin maintains its shape.

Preheat the oven to 425 degrees. On a lightly floured surface, roll out the puff pastry to about a ¼-inch thickness. Set the tenderloin in the center of the pastry and fold over the longer sides, trimming if necessary, until they slightly overlap. Brush the edges with the egg and press together to seal. Repeat with the short ends to completely seal the tenderloin. Season with coarse sea salt. Place the beef seam side down on a baking sheet. Brush the top of the pastry with the egg, then make a couple of slits in the top of the pastry.

Bake for 40 to 45 minutes or until the pastry is golden brown and the beef registers 125 degrees on an instant-read thermometer. Remove from the oven and let stand for 15 minutes before cutting into thick slices.

Beat the eggs and milk together in a stainless steel mixing bowl. Combine the dry ingredients with the wet ingredients and whisk smooth.

Whisk in the melted butter and let rest in the refrigerator for 1 hour. Bring a pot of salted water to a boil.

Working in batches, pass the batter through a spaetzle maker* into the boiling water. Cook until the spaetzle float. Remove the spaetzle using a handled strainer or spider and place into a bowl of ice water to shock. Strain spaetzle from ice water and toss lightly with olive oil. Reserve until ready to use.

If you don't have a spaetzle maker, substitute a grater, strainer or ladle with ¼-inch holes.

CHAMPIONSHIP FILET WITH GRITS, BACON JAM, AND MORELS

NICK ZOTOS,
MIKE SHANNON'S STEAKS AND SEAFOOD

SERVES 2

8 cups chicken stock

2 cups fine white polenta

2 cups Heartland Creamy goat cheese

2 tablespoons kosher salt

1 tablespoon freshly ground black pepper

½ tablespoon freshly ground white pepper

2 tablespoons unsalted butter

2 ounces fresh morel mushrooms

½ cup bacon jam (recipe follows)

2 8-ounce center-cut grass-fed beef filets

2 port-glazed shallots (recipe follows)

In a large saucepan, bring the chicken stock to a boil. Slowly whisk in the polenta little by little. Continue to stir until the polenta starts to pull away from the pan. Add in the goat cheese. Season with kosher salt and peppers. The grits should be smooth and creamy. If they are slightly lumpy, add more chicken stock.

In a medium sauté pan, heat the butter until bubbly and hot. Add the morels and swirl to coat with butter. Add 3 tablespoons of bacon jam and cook for 5 to 8 minutes over medium heat. Reserve.

Heat the grill and season the filets with salt and pepper. Grill them to your desired temperature, then allow to rest 5 minutes.

To serve, place a serving of grits in the center of two plates and top with a filet. Divide the morel mixture between the plates and place one shallot on top of the morels. With a spoon, drizzle a small amount of the port syrup around the plate.

PORT-GLAZED SHALLOTS

2 shallots, peeled and left whole

1 cup Sandeman 10-year Port

1 cup Mike Shannon's Special Reserve Cabernet

½ cup sugar

1 tablespoon whole black peppercorns

Place all of the ingredients in a small saucepan. Bring to a boil and cook for 8 minutes or until the shallots are slightly soft. Remove the shallots and reduce the liquid to a syrupy consistency. Add the shallots back to reduced syrup to glaze. Reserve for plating.

BACON JAM

½ pound applewood-smoked bacon, cut into 1-inch pieces

½ medium onion, diced

2 cloves garlic, diced

½ tablespoon brown sugar

½ tablespoon sriracha hot sauce

⅛ cup apple cider vinegar

½ cup maple syrup

1 tablespoon freshly ground black pepper

2 cups brewed coffee

Fry the bacon in a large sauté pan until slightly browned and beginning to crisp. Remove the bacon and drain off the excess grease, reserving 2 tablespoons.

Return the reserved grease to the pan, add the onion and garlic and sauté over medium heat until translucent. Add the bacon and the remaining ingredients except for the coffee. Simmer for 45 minutes, adding ½ cup of the coffee every 10 minutes. Continue to simmer, stirring occasionally. The jam is done when you can't tell the onions from the bacon. Cool completely and reserve.

CHERRY-BOURBON CHICKEN FRICASSEE

BETHANY BUDDE-COHEN, SQWIRES

SERVES 4 WITH LEFTOVERS

1 large whole fresh free-range chicken

Fresh herbs of your choice, chopped

1 tablespoon diced garlic

2 cups vegetable broth

1 cup bourbon

3 cups fresh cherries, pitted

6 large tomatoes

1 yellow pepper

1 red pepper

1 green pepper

1 large yellow onion

1 yellow squash

1 zucchini

2 tablespoons olive oil

Brown rice

Preheat the oven to 325 degrees.

Clean and rinse the chicken, then rub the skin with the herbs and garlic. Place the chicken in a roasting pan and add the vegetable broth, bourbon, and cherries. Cover the pan and roast for 2 ½ hours. When the chicken is done, allow it to cool and pull all the meat from the chicken. Discard the skin and bones.

While the chicken is cooking, chop and purée the tomatoes. Thinly slice the peppers, onion and squash.

In a large sauté pan, heat the oil. Add the onion and sauté until translucent. Add the pulled chicken and any liquid left in the roasting pan. Add the tomato purée, squash and peppers. Simmer, covered, for 35 minutes. Serve over brown rice.

CREOLE CHICKEN CLEMENCEAU

STEVE DANEY,
RIVERBEND RESTAURANT

SERVES 4

8 tablespoons butter (1 stick), divided

3 medium potatoes, peeled and cubed

3 8-ounce boneless, skinless chicken breasts, cubed*

Creole seasoning

½ cup white wine

2 tablespoons garlic, chopped

2 cups mushrooms, sliced

1 cup frozen green peas

Salt

Pepper

Melt 4 tablespoons of the butter in a large sauté pan.

CONTINUED ON PG. 64

Pan-Roasted Chicken with Tadig and Braised Leeks

CHRISTOPHER LEE, SANCTUARIA WILD TAPAS AND CAFÉ VENTANA

SERVES 4

2 Meyer lemons

½ teaspoon grated fresh ginger

3 to 4 tablespoons extra virgin olive oil

2 medium leeks, beards and green parts cut off, then quartered lengthwise (keep them as whole as possible)

¼ cup water

Salt and pepper, to taste

Tadig (recipe follows)

2 tablespoons vegetable oil

4 4-ounce chicken breasts seasoned with salt and pepper

4 tablespoons toasted, slivered or chopped almonds

TADIG

5 cups salted water

2 cups basmati rice

1 to 2 teaspoons salt

2 tablespoons olive oil

3 tablespoons butter

1 pinch saffron

The rice portion of this dish is called tadig (tah-dheeg), or Persian-style basmati. The crisp texture and buttery flavor add depth to this simple dish.

Zest the lemons until you have ½ teaspoon zest. Juice the lemons into a small bowl and add the zest, ginger, and olive oil, whisking to combine. Reserve.

Preheat the oven to 400 degrees. Place the leeks in an ovenproof pan, season to taste with salt and pepper, and add the water. Roast for 15 to 20 minutes or until the leeks are tender and fragrant.

Prepare the tadig (recipe follows).

While the rice and leeks are cooking, heat a medium skillet over medium-high heat and add the vegetable oil. When the oil is shimmery, add the chicken breasts, skin side down. Sear for about 4 to 5 minutes and turn over. Place the skillet in the oven and roast for about 5 to 10 minutes or until the chicken reads 155 degrees on a meat thermometer.

To serve, lay a mound of crispy rice down the center of a serving plate and top with the leeks. Sprinkle with toasted almonds and dress with half of the lemon vinaigrette. Place the chicken on the plate and add additional vinaigrette.

To make the tadig: Place the water in a heavy-bottomed pot and add the rice and salt. Bring to a boil and boil for 5 minutes. Then pour the rice out into a colander and rinse with cold water until the rice runs clear.

Return the pot to the stove over medium heat. Add the oil and swirl until it coats the bottom of the pot. In a separate pot, melt the butter and saffron together. Add the rinsed rice to the pot with the oil and pour the butter mixture over the rice. Place three damp paper towels over the rice and cover with a lid.

Cook over medium-high heat for 5 minutes, then turn the heat down as low as it will go and continue cooking for 15 to 20 minutes. Remove the lid and paper towels from the rice and toss.

Add the potatoes and cook over medium-high heat until they are lightly browned but not too soft. Remove from the pan and set aside.

Season the chicken to taste with the Creole seasoning. Melt the remaining 4 tablespoons of butter in a large sauté pan. Add the chicken and cook over medium heat for at least 5 minutes or until done. Add the wine, garlic, and potatoes. Stir, cover, and cook for another 5 minutes. The potatoes should be almost soft and the wine should be reduced. Uncover, add the mushrooms, and sauté until the mushrooms are soft. Add the peas and cook until heated through. Stir until well-blended, being careful not to mash the vegetables. Add salt and pepper to taste.

This dish can be made with 2 pounds of small shrimp replacing the chicken.

DUCK BREAST

RICH LORUSSO, LORUSSO'S CUCINA

SERVES 4

1 ½ pounds duck breasts

Salt and pepper, to taste

2 to 3 tablespoons olive oil

¼ pounds cipollini onions

¼ pounds Amarena cherries*

½ cup Pinot Noir

¼ cup chicken stock

¼ cup beef stock

Butter

Trim each breast until you have just enough skin to cover the top of it. Score the skin without cutting through it. Season with salt and pepper.

Preheat the oven to 350 degrees. In a skillet over medium-high heat, heat the olive oil until very hot. Sear the duck breasts skin side down until the skin is well browned. Place in a baking pan and finish in the oven for 7 minutes for medium rare.

Drain off most of the oil from the skillet and return it to the stove. Add the cipollini onions and Amarena cherries. Deglaze the pan with the wine and then add the chicken and beef stock. Season to taste with salt and pepper. Cook on medium to low heat until the sauce is reduced by half. Add a pat of butter just before serving.

Available at Whole Foods

HERB-MARINATED CHICKEN BREAST

JENNIFER PENSONEAU, JFIRES' MARKET BISTRO

SERVES 8

2 sprigs oregano

6 sprigs thyme

1 ½-inch piece rosemary

2 to 3 sprigs parsley

6 basil leaves

2 sage leaves

1 teaspoon garlic, minced

1 teaspoon shallots, minced

2 teaspoons Dijon mustard

¼ cup red wine vinegar

1 cup vegetable oil

Salt and pepper

2 pounds skinless, boneless chicken breasts, pounded to ¼-inch thickness

Preheat the oven to 350 degrees. Wash and dry the herbs. Chop the oregano, thyme, rosemary, and parsley. Chiffonade the basil and sage leaves.

In a small stainless-steel mixing bowl, combine the garlic, shallots, and Dijon mustard. Whisk in the red wine vinegar. In a fine stream, add the oil, whisking continuously. Add all of the herbs, whisk together and season to taste with salt and pepper. Set aside.

Trim the chicken breasts into 8-ounce portions and place in a nonreactive container large enough to hold all of the chicken and the marinade. Pour the marinade over the chicken and cover. Refrigerate for at least 4 hours and up to 2 days.

Heat the grill. Remove the chicken from the marinade, allowing the marinade to drain off for 30 seconds, and place on the hottest section of the grill. Top the chicken with the herbs from the marinade and cover with an inverted sauté pan. Cook for 3 to 4 minutes. Remove the herbs, flip the chicken over and cook until it registers 165 degrees, about 7 to 9 minutes total.

GUAJILLO CHICKEN

TOM SUTCLIFFE, PRIME 1000

SERVES 4

- 4 ears yellow sweet corn
- 1 package dried Guajillo chiles
- 4 8-ounce boneless chicken breasts, skin on
- 4 avocados, divided
- 3 limes, divided
- Salt, to taste
- 3 yellow peppers
- 3 red peppers
- Pepper, to taste

- 4 scallions
- 16 sprigs cilantro

Preheat the oven to 350 degrees. Place the corn, husks on, directly onto the oven rack and roast for 30 minutes. Allow to cool, husk the corn and cut the kernels off of the cobs. Keep the oven on.

In a blender, blend the chiles into a coarse purée. Wash and trim the chicken breasts, then lightly coat them with the chile purée and transfer to a baking dish. Roast for 10 to 15 minutes or until fully cooked.

Meanwhile, rinse the blender and add two avocados and add the juice of two limes. Purée until smooth, adding water until the mixture spins, if necessary. Add salt to taste and set aside.

Chop the red and yellow peppers and char in a hot skillet or under the broiler. Season to taste with salt and pepper and add them to the roasted corn. Dice remaining two avocados and toss with the roasted corn. Add lime juice, as needed, and season to taste with salt and pepper. Separately, slice the scallions and toss them with the cilantro. Paint the plate with the avocado purée. Slice the chicken and place on top. Top with avocado and corn salsa and garnish with the cilantro mixture.

ROASTED CHICKEN

CASSY VIRES, HOME WINE KITCHEN

SERVES 4

- 1 small, 3- to 4-pound chicken, halved
- 12 shallots, thinly sliced
- 6 sprigs fresh oregano
- 6 fresh lemon leaves*

CONTINUED ON PG. 68

RICH LORUSSO,
LORUSSO'S CUCINA

Your favorite cookbook? *The Silver Spoon.*

One great cooking tip? Caramelization of your ingredients.

Your favorite five-ingredient dish? Lasagna.

Which dish does your family ask you to make? Soup. I usually make a vegetable with beans.

Chicken Spiedini with Wild Mushroom Risotto

RICH LORUSSO, LORUSSO'S CUCINA

SERVES 4

3 to 4 shallots

⅔ cup Italian bread crumbs, plus extra for breading

¼ cup diced sun-dried tomatoes

4 ounces herbed goat cheese

1 pound boneless, skinless chicken breasts, pounded thin

Wild mushroom risotto (recipe follows)

Preheat the oven to 350 degrees.

Peel the shallots, drizzle with olive oil and roast on a baking sheet for 30 minutes. When they are cool enough to handle, dice the shallots. Combine ⅔ cup diced roasted shallots with ⅔ cup Italian breadcrumbs, the sun-dried tomatoes, and goat cheese. Leave the oven on.

Spread a spoonful of stuffing on each chicken breast. Roll up the breasts, starting at the pointed end of each piece, and secure with skewers. Then baste each piece with olive oil and roll in additional breadcrumbs to coat.

Grill or sauté the chicken breasts until brown. Finish in the oven for 6 minutes. Let rest for 5 minutes. Cut each breast in half to serve.

WILD MUSHROOM RISOTTO

2 cups Arborio rice

4 ½ cups vegetable stock

1 ½ cups wild mushrooms, chopped

½ cup sweet Marsala wine

Pinch saffron

3 tablespoons softened butter

½ cup grated Parmesan cheese

Cook the rice in the vegetable stock, following the directions on the package. Halfway through the cooking time, add the wild mushrooms, Marsala wine, and saffron. When the rice is cooked, stir in the butter and Parmesan cheese.

Serve immediately with the chicken spiedini.

BEN LESTER, MOSAIC

Who taught you to cook? My family and every chef, cook, dishwasher, and server I've ever worked with.

Your favorite comfort food? Biscuits & gravy, with chicken and dumplings being a close second!

Your favorite restaurant in town (aside from your own)? I Fratellini.

Pancetta-Wrapped Quail

BEN LESTER, MOSAIC

SERVES 2

4 quail, semi-boneless

3 ounces Italian pancetta, sliced thin

2 ounces Spanish Manchego, cut in four 2 by ¼-inch logs

1 teaspoon Ras el Hanout*

2 French Horn Mushrooms (or another meaty mushroom, such as portobello)

¼ pound sugar snap peas, split open at the seam

2 cups homemade chicken stock or buy chicken glace from specialty grocers. Do not use boullion

1 tablespoon unsalted butter

4 cloves garlic

1 teaspoon kosher salt

½ teaspoon fresh ground black pepper

*Moroccan spice blend found at specialty grocers

MUSHROOM MARINADE

3 tablespoons extra virgin olive oil

1 tablespoon fresh orange juice

½ tablespoon lemon juice

1 tablespoon red wine vinegar

¼ tablespoon kosher salt

1 pinch ground black pepper

Take the four quail, pat dry with paper towels, and lay flat on a cutting board, skin side down. Cut off the small wing bones and reserve for sauce. Spread out the quail and lightly flatten the meat with a mallet, taking care not to rip the skin or flesh. Season the quail evenly across the surface with a pinch of Ras el Hanout, salt, and pepper. Place one of the four logs of manchego on each quail. Take the edge of the quail and roll over the manchego up towards the leg bone. Take the thin sliced pancetta and wrap around the quail to secure the roll. Once rolled, season the outside of the quail with another small pinch of Ras el Hanout, salt, and pepper. Cover with plastic wrap and place in fridge until ready to cook.

Preheat outdoor grill or cast iron grill pan to medium high.

Following directions of a stovetop or outdoor smoker, lightly smoke the garlic cloves for 8-10 minutes until golden and barely tender. In a small saucepot, add the chicken stock and smoked garlic and bring to a simmer. Reduce until slightly thickened. Remove the cloves of garlic, season with salt and pepper if needed, and keep warm.

Mix the marinade ingredients together in a non-reactive bowl. Slice the mushrooms in half longways and toss together with marinade. Place into fridge for 20 to 30 minutes; giving them a toss halfway through.

Grill the quail 4 to 5 minutes on each side. Check occasionally to make sure the pancetta does not burn. When the quail are halfway done, wipe off excess marinade and grill 1 to 2 minutes per side depending on size. Rewarm the chicken stock if necessary and stir in ½ tablespoon butter. Heat a sauté pan over med-high heat and add remaining ½ tablespoon butter. Once melted, add the split sugar snap peas and toss two or three times to expose all sides to the butter. Season with a pinch of salt and pepper and remove to a plate. Peas should stay bright green and crunchy.

Spoon sauce onto plates, lay the mushroom cut side up on top of the sauce. Place sugar snap peas around the mushroom and rest the quail on top.

before it is time to serve the dish, place the polenta on an oiled pan in the oven until it is browned on the bottom. Carefully take the cakes off with a spatula.

Available at Williams Brothers Meat Market

PORK-SHOULDER BURGERS

ANTHONY DEVOTI, FIVE BISTRO

SERVES 6

Olive oil

3 shallots, finely diced

1 stalk celery, finely diced

2 cloves garlic, minced

3 cups shredded braised or roasted pork shoulder

2 eggs

½ cup breadcrumbs

Salt and pepper, to taste

Thinly sliced bacon

Spicy barbecue sauce (recipe follows)

Coat a small sauté pan with olive oil and heat until hot. Add the shallots, celery, and garlic and cook over medium heat until the shallots are translucent.

In a bowl, combine the meat, cooked vegetables, eggs, and breadcrumbs. Add salt and pepper lightly throughout the mixing process. This mixture should resemble the consistency of a meatloaf: it should be slightly dry, not wet, but should have a nice sheen.

Using a 1-ounce ice cream scoop, make the mixture into balls. Wrap these individually in bacon. In a hot sauté pan, sear each side until the bacon is crisp. Drain on paper towels and set aside.

Warm the barbecue sauce. Add the seared bacon-wrapped burgers and simmer over low heat for about an hour. Serve.

SPICY BARBECUE SAUCE

2 tablespoons vegetable oil

1 medium onion, finely chopped

⅓ cup celery, chopped

1 tablespoon garlic, minced

1 tablespoon paprika

½ teaspoon cayenne pepper

¼ cup ketchup

½ cup beer

½ cup apple cider vinegar

1 tablespoon Worcestershire sauce

3 cups pork or chicken stock

Heat the oil in a heavy medium-sized saucepan over medium heat. Add the onion and celery and sauté until tender, about 5 minutes. Add the garlic, paprika, and cayenne, and stir for 1 minute. Add the ketchup, beer, vinegar, Worcestershire sauce, and stock. Reduce the heat to medium-low and simmer uncovered until the flavors blend and the sauce is reduced by half, stirring occasionally.

POLENTA WITH SAUSAGE

DOMINIC GALATI, DOMINIC'S ON THE HILL, DOMINIC'S TRATTORIA, AND GIO'S RISTORANTE & BAR

SERVES 4

3 tablespoons butter

½ cup onion or shallots, chopped

½ cup Italian sausage, chopped

4 cups water or chicken broth, divided

1 cup dry polenta

2 tablespoons to ½ cup grated
  Parmesan cheese

½ cup grated mozzarella cheese

Salt and pepper, to taste

In a large saucepot, melt the butter. Add the onions and sausage and sauté until the onions are translucent. Add 3 cups water or chicken broth and bring to a boil. Moisten the polenta with 1 cup water or chicken stock, then add it to the sausage mixture and stir to combine. Stir in the cheese, and season to taste with salt and pepper.

At this point, the polenta can be transferred to a baking sheet or loaf pan and chilled until firm, which will allow you to cut it into slices and prepare to your liking: baked, fried, or sautéed.

PORK TACOS

REX HALE, THREE SIXTY

SERVES 4

1 pound pulled pork shoulder

Korean barbecue sauce, to taste (recipe
  follows)

12 2 ½-inch flour tortillas

2 cups kimchi (recipe follows)

1 cup pickled cucumber (recipe follows)

Daikon sprouts

Heat the pork in the barbecue sauce, stirring gently until heated through. Warm the tortillas, then divide the pork between them. Top with kimchi and pickled cucumbers, and then garnish with daikon sprouts.

KOREAN BARBECUE SAUCE

½ cup Korean fermented hot pepper sauce

¾ cup plus 1 tablespoon sugar

¾ cup soy sauce

4 teaspoons rice wine vinegar

4 teaspoons sesame oil

Combine all of the ingredients in a stockpot and bring to a quick simmer. Remove from the heat. Chill.

PICKLED CUCUMBER

1 English cucumber, peeled, seeded, and
  thinly sliced

2 tablespoons rice wine vinegar

2 tablespoons sugar

½ teaspoon serrano chile, seeded and minced

2 teaspoons sea salt

Place all the ingredients in a container and chill for several hours.

KIMCHI

1 head green cabbage, about 1 pound,
  finely shredded

2 ounces sea salt

½ cup rice wine vinegar

1 tablespoon sugar

2 tablespoons sriracha hot chile sauce

1-inch piece fresh ginger, peeled and grated

2 cloves garlic, minced

2 scallions, sliced thin on a bias

2 carrots, julienned

¼ cup soy sauce

2 tablespoons sesame oil

Toss the cabbage in the salt and set in a colander. Allow to wilt for about 2 hours.

In the meantime, mix together all of the remaining

Goat milk (skim milk may be substituted)

2 eggs

Olive oil

Toast and grind the juniper berries.

Cut the goat and fat into pieces that will fit into your grinder. Chill the goat meat until very cold and firm. Chill the fat until nearly frozen. Grind the meat and fat through a ¼-inch plate and keep chilled in the bowl of the mixer.

Add the remaining ingredients, except the wine, bread, milk, and eggs. Mix on low speed for 2 minutes. Add the wine and continue mixing on low speed until the wine is absorbed. Then turn up the speed to medium and process for 1 minute. Remove from the bowl and chill very well. (At this point, you have a great mild sausage that you can use for sausages or for grilling on skewers.)

To make the meatballs, place the bread in a bowl and cover it with milk. Press it and squeeze it to break up the chunks. Let soak for 30 minutes in the refrigerator. Squeeze out the milk and place the bread in the bowl of a food processor with the sausage. Add the eggs. Process by pulsing on and off until the mixture is well incorporated and somewhat smooth. Cook a small sample in the microwave briefly on low and adjust the seasoning, if needed.

Chill for 2 hours to firm up. Scoop the meatball mixture for your preferred size. Lightly grease your hands with extra-virgin olive oil and roll the meatball in your hands. Coat a sauté pan with olive oil and heat until hot. Add the meatballs and cook until browned.

Available at Jones Heritage Farms. Ask for Gerry.

LAMB SHANK WITH ROASTED BABY BEETS AND GREENS, WHITE BEANS AND HORSERADISH CRÈME FRAÎCHE

KRIS JANIK, FRANCO

SERVES 4

4 lamb shanks

Salt and pepper, to taste

2 ribs celery

1 carrot

1 onion

2 cups dried white beans

1 sprig sage

2 bay leaves

1 bunch baby beets

½ cup olive oil

½ cup sherry vinegar

4 sprigs thyme

3 cloves garlic, smashed

Salt and pepper, to taste

1 cup tomato paste

½ cup prepared horseradish

1 cup crème fraîche

2 tablespoons Dijon mustard

Juice of 1 lemon

Season the lamb with salt and pepper and let sit for a couple of hours.

Preheat the oven to 350 degrees.

Peel the celery, carrot and onion, chop them coarsely and toss them with the tomato paste. Combine the vegetables and the lamb in a covered baking dish. Bake, covered, for 4 hours or until tender. When cool, remove the meat off the bones, strain any liquid from the braising pan and set aside.

Make a stock: Add the bones to a small pot, like a 4-quart saucepan. Cover with water and simmer for 2 hours or so. Strain and reduce by half. The liquid reserved from the braising pan can then be added and reduced if needed. Seasoning can be adjusted with salt, lemon juice, or vinegar.

ROASTED BABY BEETS

Preheat the oven to 350.

Trim the tops off the beets. Reserve. Place the beets in a pan that can be covered and add the oil, vinegar, thyme, and garlic. Season to taste with salt and pepper. Bake for 1 hour to 1½ hours. Let cool. Then peel and quarter the beets.

For the beet greens: Bring a pot of water to a boil and season well with salt. Have a bowl of ice water ready to shock the greens. Blanch the greens until tender. Do it in batches if your pot is small. Remove and shock in the ice water. Remove from the ice water soon after cooling.

WHITE BEANS

Soak the beans and herbs in enough water to cover by a couple of inches for several hours or overnight. To cook, place all of the beans in a large pot and cover with more water, if needed. Simmer until tender. Let cool and keep them in the cooking liquid.

Heat the beans in their cooking liquid, adding 1 tablespoon of olive oil. When they are warmed and the liquid begins to reduce, season to taste with salt and pepper. The idea is to create an emulsification.

Preheat the oven to 500 degrees. Combine the lamb meat and the reduced stock in a roasting pan and simmer in the oven, occasionally spooning the sauce over the meat, until it is nice and glazed. It should take about 10 to 15 minutes. When the lamb looks kind of shiny and delicious, you know it's ready.

This can be plated for each person or served family style with the horseradish on the side.

HORSERADISH CRÈME FRAÎCHE

Combine all of the ingredients and let sit for a while to allow the flavors to develop.

ROASTED AND SLOW-STEWED LAMB

CARY McDOWELL, WINSLOW'S HOME

SERVES 4

You can use a combination of lamb cuts in this recipe. I suggest you take a trip to a local farmers' market, where you'll find a couple of local farmers of merit who provide wonderful, fresh, mindfully raised lamb.

Like pot roast, this dish tastes better the next day, so for best results, prepare the dish a day in advance. Gently reheat it before serving either on the stovetop or in the microwave.

6 pounds lamb (maybe a mixture of shoulder
    and leg), bone-in
Salt and pepper
1 large onion
2 stalks celery
1 carrot
1 parsnip
1 fennel bulb
Olive oil
12 large garlic cloves, peeled and smashed
Red wine (something cheap and balanced),
    enough to completely cover the vegetables
    and lamb

CONTINUED ON PG. 80

Parmesan-Crusted Lamb Chops

VINCE BOMMARITO JR., TONY'S

SERVES 4

12 single lamb rib
chops, partly boned
and flattened

½ cup freshly grated
Parmesan cheese,
spread on a dish or
waxed paper

3 eggs, lightly beaten

1 cup fine unflavored
bread crumbs, spread
on a dish or waxed
paper

Olive oil, enough to
come up ¼ inch of the
skillet

Salt

Freshly ground pepper,
about six twists of the
mill

Turn both sides of the lamb chops in the Parmesan cheese, then give the chops a tap to shake off the excess. Dip them immediately into the beaten eggs, letting any excess egg flow back into the dish. Then turn the chops in the breadcrumbs, coating both sides and tapping them again to shake off all the excess. (You can prepare the chops up to this point as much as an hour ahead of time, or if you refrigerate them, even 3 or 4 hours. If refrigerated, return to room temperature before frying.)

Heat the oil in a large skillet over medium heat until it is very hot. Fry as many chops at one time as will fit loosely in the skillet. As soon as they have formed a nice crust on one side, season with salt and pepper and turn them. Add salt and pepper to the other side. Transfer to a warm platter as soon as the second side has formed a crust. Proceed to the next batch.

Serve with lemon wedges or top with arugula that is dressed with balsamic vinegar and olive oil.

3 large tomatoes

Chicken stock

Preheat the oven to 300 degrees. Put a cast-iron or enameled covered casserole dish on stove to preheat as well. Season the lamb's surface aggressively with salt and pepper and set aside.

Cut the onion, celery, carrot, parsnip, and fennel into dime-sized pieces and set aside.

Coat the preheated casserole dish with oil and heat over medium-high heat. Add the lamb and sear it on all sides, creating a browned crust. Remove and set aside. Add all of the cut vegetables and the garlic to the casserole dish and stir. Cover and cook for 3 to 5 minutes or until the vegetables are soft and slightly browned. Add the red wine and cook until it is reduced by 75 percent. Add the tomatoes.

Return the meat to the casserole dish and add enough chicken stock to cover the meat. Cover and place in the oven. Bake for 3 to 4 hours or until the meat is tender. Remove. Cool to room temperature.

When cool, remove the meat from the bone, making sure no bones or connective tissue remains, and place it in a suitable casserole dish. Pour the cooking liquid through a large strainer, then a small one, making sure to press enough pulp through to thicken the sauce. Pour the sauce over the meat and place in the refrigerator to chill fully. This can be served hot or at room temperature.

LAMB MEATBALLS WITH ROASTED FINGERLING POTATOES AND ZUCCHINI

VITO RACANELLI, MAD TOMATO

SERVES 4

- 3 tablespoons olive oil
- 1 cup onions, chopped
- 1 tablespoon garlic, chopped
- 10 basil leaves
- 10 to 12 fingerling potatoes, cut in half lengthwise
- 2 cups white wine
- 3 cups San Marzano tomatoes, crushed by hand
- 8 to 10 lamb meatballs (recipe follows)
- 1 cup water
- 1 large zucchini, deseeded and diced large
- Salt and pepper, to taste

Preheat the oven to 400 degrees.

In a large sauté pan, heat the olive oil. Add the onions and sauté until lightly cooked. Add the garlic, basil, and potatoes and cook for a minute more. Deglaze the pan with the white wine. Add tomatoes.

Place the meatballs in a roasting pan. Pour in the sauce from the deglazed pan and the water. Add the zucchini and season to taste with salt and pepper. Bake for 35 minutes.

LAMB MEATBALLS

- 2 pounds ground lamb
- 2 eggs
- 6 ounces spinach, blanched and chopped
- 1 fresh basil leaves, chopped
- 5 ounces goat cheese

5 ounces grated Parmesan

5 ounces breadcrumbs

1 teaspoon garlic, chopped

Salt and pepper, to taste

Preheat the oven to 350 degrees.

Using the paddle attachment on a stand mixer, mix all of the ingredients together until well blended. Roll the mixture into 4- to 5-ounce balls, making sure the balls are rolled tightly without cracks. Place balls on a baking sheet and bake them for 35 minutes. Remove and cool.

TALEGGIO CHEESE AGNOLOTTI, LOCAL OYSTER MUSHROOMS, AND MISSOURI PECANS WITH TRUFFLE HONEY

CHRIS BORK, BLOOD & SAND

SERVES 8

2 tablespoons vegetable oil

1 cup oyster mushrooms

Salt and pepper, to taste

½ cup vegetable stock

¼ cup (½ stick) cold butter

1 sprig fresh thyme

Taleggio cheese agnolotti (recipe follows)

¼ cup toasted pecans

Truffle honey (recipe follows)

Heat a large sauté skillet over high heat. Add the oil and mushrooms, season to taste with salt and pepper, and sauté until golden brown. Add the vegetable stock, butter and thyme. Boil so the stock reduces and emulsifies with the butter. Once the sauce has thickened, remove it from the heat.

Bring a pot of salted water to a boil. Add the agnolotti and cook until they float. Drain, then add the pasta to the sauce and gently toss.

Divide onto serving plates, top with pecans and drizzle with truffle honey.

TALEGGIO CHEESE AGNOLOTTI

10 ounces Taleggio cheese, trimmed of rind

2 cups cream

¼ cup white wine

1 tablespoon salt

¼ teaspoon black pepper

1 ½ teaspoons milk

1 ½ eggs

9 egg yolks

2 ¾ cups all-purpose flour

3 teaspoons extra-virgin olive oil

Let the cheese come to room temperature. In separate pots, reduce the cream and the white wine by half. In a blender or food processor, combine the cheese, salt, and pepper with the wine and cream while still hot and purée until smooth. Transfer to a piping bag and place in the refrigerator.

Whisk together the milk, eggs, and egg yolks. In the bowl of a stand mixer, stir the flour with a dough hook and slowly add the olive oil. Add the milk mixture and knead in the bowl until the dough is very smooth, about 5 minutes. Refrigerate for at least an hour.

Remove the pasta dough from the fridge and cut into four pieces. Keep the dough covered or it will dry out. Flatten the quarter of dough with your hands or a rolling pin. It needs to fit through the pasta roller at its number 1 setting. Lightly flour your dough and pass it through the pasta roller twice on each setting

CONTINUED ON PG. 84

Braised Lamb Shanks

JIM FIALA, THE CROSSING, LILUMA, LILUMA'S SIDE DOOR, AND ACERO
SERVES 6

Salt and freshly ground
  black pepper
6 lamb shanks
Extra virgin olive oil
3 medium yellow onions,
  diced
2 cups celery, diced
2 cups carrots, diced
3 cloves garlic, diced
  cup tomato paste
1 cup white wine
½ sprig thyme
½ sprig rosemary
1 pound baby artichokes
3 tablespoons extra virgin
  olive oil
Salt and pepper, to taste

Preheat the oven to 350 degrees.

Salt and pepper the lamb shanks and rub with a little oil. Brown in a heavy pan over medium-high heat, making sure not to move the shanks too much to ensure browning on all sides. Remove the shanks and set aside.

Add the onions, celery, carrots, and garlic to the pan. Scrape all the brown bits off the bottom of the pan while sweating the vegetables.

Add the tomato paste and wine to the vegetables and cook for about 2 minutes. Add the herbs and nestle the lamb shanks in the vegetables about half way up the lamb shanks. Lightly cover and cook in the oven until the liquid is just bubbling and the meat starts to loosen from the bone. Remove the lamb and set on a tray.

Run the vegetables and liquid from the pan through a food mill. Watch for bones, as they can wreck a food mill. Strain the liquid through a chinois and heat to a sauce-like consistency.

For the baby artichokes: Preheat oven to 350 degrees.

Trim the outer, green leaves from the artichoke, until you reach the soft, yellow leaves. Cut the tops off and trim the stem. Cut each cleaned artichoke in half and toss together in a bowl with the olive oil, salt, and pepper. Spread the artichokes onto a baking sheet, in a single layer, and roast in the oven for 25 to 30 minutes.

To serve, place each shank on a plate with roasted baby artichokes. Spoon a little of the sauce on top of the shanks and drizzle the shanks and artichokes with a little extra virgin olive oil.

starting from one to four. Pipe a heaped tablespoon of the cheese filling on the middle of the sheet a ½ inch apart. Brush some egg wash on the pasta around each portion of cheese. Fold the sheet over the cheese and seal the pasta around the cheese with your fingers ensuring there are no air pockets. Cut around the filling leaving some pasta.

TRUFFLE HONEY

> 1 tablespoon truffle oil
> ¼ cup local honey
> Pinch black pepper

Whisk the oil into the honey until emulsified. Add pepper and whisk to combine.

PASTA WITH CAULIFLOWER

MICHAEL DEL PIETRO, SUGO'S SPAGHETTERIA, PAZZO'S PIZZERIA, BABBO'S SPAGHETTERIA, TAVOLO V, AND VIA VINO ENOTECA

SERVES 4

> 2 tablespoons olive oil
> 3 ½ cups cauliflower, chopped
> 1 small yellow onion, finely chopped
> Heavy pinch salt
> Heavy pinch pepper
> 1 teaspoon garlic, minced
> 2 tablespoons salted butter, divided
> 2 cups vegetable stock
> 10 ounces dry pasta, cooked and drained
> ½ cup flat-leaf parsley, chopped

In a large pot, heat the olive oil. Add the cauliflower and onions and sauté for 5 to 7 minutes. Season with salt and pepper. Add the garlic and 1 tablespoon of butter. Add the vegetable stock and cook for 5 minutes to reduce. Add the cooked pasta, parsley and remaining butter. Cook for 2 minutes and serve.

PASTA FUNGHI

MICHAEL DEL PIETRO, SUGO'S SPAGHETTERIA, PAZZO'S PIZZERIA, BABBO'S SPAGHETTERIA, TAVOLO V, AND VIA VINO ENOTECA

SERVES 2

> 3 tablespoons olive oil
> 4 tablespoons butter, divided
> 10 ounces fresh mushrooms, such as portobellos, shiitakes, and domestic, chopped
> 1 to 2 cloves garlic, minced
> 2 pinches each salt and pepper, divided
> 2 cups mushroom or vegetable stock
> 6 ounces dried pasta, cooked al dente
> 2 ounces fresh spinach
> Parmigiano-Reggiano

In a large sauce pot, heat the olive oil and 2 tablespoons of butter. Add the mushrooms and sauté for about 3 minutes. Add the garlic, 1 pinch of salt and 1 pinch of pepper. Cook for another 2 minutes.

Add the mushroom stock and bring to a simmer. Cook down for about 5 minutes

Add the cooked pasta, fresh spinach, 1 pinch of salt, 1 pinch of pepper, and the remaining 2 tablespoons of butter. Toss to combine.

Divide into serving bowls and top with a freshly grated Parmigiano-Reggiano cheese.

CLASSIC CHEESE FONDUE

MARC FELIX, CONSULTING CHEF

SERVES 4

- ¾ pound Gruyère
- ¾ pound Emmentaler
- 1 tablespoon cornstarch
- 1 clove garlic
- 1 cup dry white wine
- 3 tablespoons Kirschwasser
- 1 loaf French bread, cubed

Grate the cheese into a bowl. Sprinkle with the cornstarch and toss to coat.

Peel the garlic and cut it in half lengthwise. Rub the inside of a cooking pot with the cut surface of the garlic. Discard the garlic.

Add the wine to the pot and heat over medium heat until bubbles just begin to break the surface. Do not boil.

Add the cheese one handful at a time, stirring continually until each addition is melted and smooth. Do not let it come to a boil.

Add the Kirschwasser to the cheese fondue while stirring.

Light the candle or burner in a fondue stand. Pour the cheese mixture into the fondue pot and set it over the burner, adjusting the heat so the cheese does not burn. Serve immediately with the French bread.

RIGATONI ALLA NORMA

PAUL MANNO, PAUL MANNO'S CAFE

SERVES 3 TO 4

This is one of the most famous pasta dishes in all of Sicily— no one is sure who Norma is, but you'll find this dish prepared in just about every restaurant and household.

- Extra-virgin olive oil
- 4 cloves garlic, roughly chopped
- 3 shallots, roughly chopped
- 1 28-ounce can San Marzano plum tomatoes
- ½ bunch fresh basil (or more, to taste), roughly chopped
- 1 large or 2 small eggplant(s)
- Salt
- Vegetable oil
- 1 cup flour
- 1 box rigatoni
- Parmigiano-Reggiano
- Ricotta salata

Coat a medium stockpot with olive oil and heat over medium heat until hot. Add the garlic and shallots and sauté until they turn a light brown color. In a food processor, pulse the tomatoes into medium-small chunks. Add the tomatoes and the basil to the pot and cook over medium heat for 35 to 45 minutes, stirring every 5 minutes or so. Once the sauce has reduced to your preferred consistency, remove from the heat and set aside. (You might have a thin layer of light red foam on the top. Don't stir that into the sauce; skim that off the top using a large spoon and discard.)

Cut both ends off the eggplant and trim off the skin. Cut the eggplant into medium-sized cubes. Fill a glass bowl halfway full with cold water and add a small palmful of salt. Stir.

Shrimp, Missouri Country Ham, and Heirloom Grits with Cheddar

BILL CARDWELL, CARDWELL'S AT THE PLAZA AND BC'S KITCHEN

SERVES 8

2 pounds large shrimp in shell

4 tablespoons olive oil, divided

1 large onion, minced

2 celery stalks, minced

4 large cloves garlic, minced

4 sprigs fresh thyme

4 sprigs fresh tarragon

2 bay leaves

1 teaspoon Old Bay seasoning

2 tablespoons tomato paste

1 cup white wine

2 quarts water

Salt and pepper, as needed

7 tablespoons softened butter, divided

3 tablespoons flour

8 ounces Missouri Country ham, finely diced

Hot sauce (optional)

1 tablespoon sea salt

6 cups cold water

1 ¼ cups heirloom grits (available from AnsonMills.com)

1 cup shredded aged white cheddar cheese

1 cup green onions, thinly sliced

Peel and devein the shrimp, reserving the shells.

Heat 2 tablespoons of the olive oil in a heavy 4-quart saucepot. Add the reserved shrimp shells and cook, stirring, until they turn pink. Add the onion, celery, garlic, thyme, tarragon, bay leaves, and Old Bay seasoning and sauté for 2 to 3 minutes. Add the tomato paste, wine, and water. Bring to a boil, reduce the heat and simmer for 1 hour. Strain the shells and solids, reserving the stock and discarding the solids.

Place the strained stock in a saucepot and reduce to approximately 4 cups. Taste and adjust the seasoning with salt and pepper. Combine 6 tablespoons of the butter and the flour and knead into a paste. Slowly whip the paste into the stock a little at a time to thicken. Bring to a boil, reduce the heat and simmer for 10 minutes. Strain and reserve. Keep warm.

Heat the remaining 2 tablespoons olive oil in a large sauté pan. Add the ham and cook, stirring, until brown and crispy. Remove with a slotted spoon and reserve. Add the shrimp—and more oil, if needed—in a single layer and cook until pink on both sides. Remove and reserve with the ham. When all the shrimp are cooked, combine the ham and shrimp with the sauce. Adjust the seasoning, adding hot sauce to taste if desired.

In a 4-quart saucepot with a lid, bring 1 tablespoon sea salt and 6 cups of cold water to a boil. Slowly add the grits and stir until they begin to thicken. Cover, reduce the heat to low and simmer, stirring occasionally, until the grits are tender and thick. Add the cheese and remaining 1 tablespoon butter. Season to taste with salt and pepper.

To serve, portion the grits into bowls. Ladle the shrimp, ham and sauce on top. Sprinkle with green onion.

Scallops with Cauliflower Purée, Romanesco, Guanciale, and Rhubarb

GERARD CRAFT, NICHE, TASTE, BRASSERIE BY NICHE, AND PASTARIA

SERVES 8

3 tablespoons olive oil

1 large white onion, thinly sliced

2 stalks rhubarb, thinly sliced

¾ cup white wine

High-quality extra-virgin olive oil

Sugar, to taste

1 head cauliflower, chopped

2 cups milk

Salt, to taste

16 slices guanciale (available from Volpi Foods)

4 heads baby romanesco broccoli, quartered (available at Whole Foods)

16 morel mushrooms, cleaned and halved

Pepper, to taste

16 extra-large scallops (U-10), side muscle removed

3 tablespoons canola oil

In a small pot, heat the olive oil. Add the onion and rhubarb and cook until the onions are translucent. Add the white wine and cook until the liquid is almost completely reduced. Purée and add a high-quality extra virgin olive oil and a little sugar to taste.

In a medium-sized pot, combine the cauliflower and milk and simmer until the cauliflower is tender. Strain the milk and reserve. Purée the cauliflower, adding enough of the reserved milk to get a creamy consistency. Season to taste with salt. Keep warm.

Preheat the oven to 400 degrees. Place the guanciale on a cookie sheet and bake until crisp.

In a hot pan, sauté the romanesco and morels until the romanesco is tender. Add the guanciale and season to taste with salt and pepper.

Season the scallops with salt and pepper on both sides. In a saute pan, heat the canola oil, add the scallops and sauté until one side is golden. Flip and brown the other side. The scallops are done when they have just begun to firm. (If the scallops are very large, they may need to be placed in a 450-degree oven until done.)

To serve, place a puddle of cauliflower purée on a plate and top with the romanesco mixture. Put a few dots of rhubarb sauce on plate, and top it all with two scallops.

HARISSA

- ½ cup roasted red peppers
- ½ chipotle pepper
- ½ cup lime juice
- 1 clove garlic
- ¼ teaspoon coriander seed, crushed
- ½ teaspoon paprika
- ⅓ cup vegetable oil
- Salt and pepper, to taste

Place all of the ingredients except the oil into a blender. Turn it on low speed and slowly increase the speed to high. Gradually add the oil until it's emulsified. Season to taste salt and pepper.

BALSAMIC SYRUP

- ½ cup balsamic vinegar
- ¼ cup light corn syrup
- 1 tablespoon soy sauce

Combine all of the ingredients in a saucepan and bring to a boil. Reduce the heat to low and cook down until the sauce is a syrup-like consistency. Allow to cool. If it is too thick to drizzle, add a small amount of hot water and stir with a whisk.

SZECHUAN LONG BEAN DRESSING

- 2 tablespoons sambal (garlic chile paste)
- ¼ cup soy sauce
- 1 ½ tablespoons light corn syrup
- 1 tablespoon cilantro, finely chopped
- 1 ½ tablespoons sesame oil
- ¼ cup vegetable oil

Combine the first four ingredients. Slowly add the oil, whisking constantly, until the mixture is emulsified.

BLACK & BLUE MUSSELS
ERIC KELLY, SCAPE AMERICAN BISTRO
SERVES 1 TO 2

- 1 pound Prince Edward Island mussels
- 1 tablespoon olive oil
- 2 tablespoons bacon lardons
- 7 garlic cloves, roasted
- 2 tablespoons white wine
- 4 tablespoons chicken stock
- 6 tablespoons butter, diced
- 2 tablespoons blue cheese
- ½ jalapeño, sliced thin
- Wedges of crusty bread

Wash the mussels under cold running water, scrubbing away the beards.

Heat the oil in a large skillet over moderate heat. Add the bacon and garlic, and cook for 1 minute or until the bacon is golden brown. Add the mussels and cook for 1 minute or until the mussels begin to open. Add the wine and chicken stock. Bring to a boil and reduce by half. Add the butter and swirl to emulsify with the reduction.

Pour into a warm serving bowl, top with cheese and jalapeño. Serve with wedges of crusty bread.

SHRIMP AND GRITS
ERIC KELLEY,
SCAPE AMERICAN BISTRO
SERVES 4

- 12 jumbo shrimp, raw and peeled
- 1 pinch kosher salt

- 1 pinch fresh black pepper
- 1 pinch Cajun spice
- 1 tablespoon olive oil
- 1 tablespoon lemon juice
- 1 tablespoon Worcestershire sauce
- 2 tablespoons hot sauce
- ½ cup amber beer
- 8 tablespoons (1 stick) butter, diced
- 8 ounces cheddar grits (recipe follows)

Place the shrimp on a plate and season with the salt, pepper, and Cajun spice. Heat the olive oil in a pan over medium heat. Place the shrimp in the pan and cook for 1 to 2 minutes. Flip and cook for another 1 to 2 minutes. Remove and place on a paper towel-lined platter. Wipe out the pan and place it back on the stove over medium heat. Add the lemon juice, Worcestershire, hot sauce, and beer. Reduce the sauce by 85 percent, then whisk in the butter. Turn off the heat, add the shrimp to the sauce and let sit for 1 minute. To serve, place 2 ounces of cooked grits in center of each plate. Place three shrimp on top of each portion of grits. Using a spoon, drizzle the shrimp with the remaining sauce.

CHEDDAR GRITS

- 1 ¼ cups chicken stock
- 1 ¼ cups heavy cream
- ½ cup quick-cooking grits
- 1 pinch kosher salt
- 1 pinch fresh black pepper
- 4 ounces cheddar cheese, shredded
- ⅓ cup vegetable oil
- Salt and pepper, to taste

Bring the cream and stock to a simmer. Slowly add the grits to the simmering liquid, whisking constantly. Lower the heat and cook for 12 to 15 minutes. Season with salt and pepper. Stir in the cheese

CREOLE CAKES

MICHAEL RYAN, LOLA

SERVES 4 TO 6

- 1 pound claw meat crabmeat
- 6 ounces crawfish tails, chopped
- 1 green pepper, diced
- 1 red pepper, diced
- 1 small yellow onion, diced
- 1 tablespoon ground mustard
- 3 tablespoons Worcestershire sauce
- 2 tablespoons sriracha pepper sauce
- 3 eggs
- 1 cup mayonnaise
- 1 tablespoon onion powder
- ½ tablespoon garlic powder
- ½ tablespoon Cajun seasoning
- ½ tablespoon crushed red pepper
- 2 to 3 cups breadcrumbs, plus extra
  for breading
- Olive oil

In a large bowl, combine all of the ingredients except the breadcrumbs. Gradually add the breadcrumbs, using as much as necessary to make the batter pasty and it holds together.

Shape the mixture into 2-ounce portions and flatten slightly. Roll the patties in breadcrumbs to coat.

Coat a large skillet with olive oil and heat until very hot. Add the patties and fry over medium heat until golden brown. Serve with your favorite sauce.

SHRIMP SALTIMBOCCA, CANNELLINI BEANS, AND MINT OIL

FABRIZIO SCHENARDI, CIELO

SERVES 4

16 extra large shrimp, peeled, deveined, and
   butterflied

16 sage leaves

16 slices prosciutto di Parma

¾ cup ounces flour

¾ cup olive oil, divided, plus extra for
   dressing

¼ cup plus 2 tablespoons dry white wine

Black pepper, to taste

4 tablespoons butter

¾ cup chopped parsley

½ cup mint leaves

Baby arugula

Salt, to taste

Cannellini bean purée (recipe follows)

Place a sage leaf on top of each shrimp, then wrap the shrimp with the prosciutto. Lightly coat the wrapped shrimp with flour, shaking off any excess.

In a large nonstick skillet, heat ¼ cup olive oil until very hot. Add the shrimp and sauté for 2 to 3 minutes on each side. Remove the shrimp and reserve. Deglaze the pan with the white wine, then add the pepper and the butter and stir until the butter melts. Stir in the parsley.

Bring 3 cups of water to a boil in a small saucepan. Add the mint leaves and boil for 1 minute. Remove the leaves, then shock them in ice-cold water. Squeeze the water from the leaves, then place them in a food processor. With the motor running, slowly pour in ½ cup of olive oil and process until emulsified.

Toss the baby arugula with a drizzle of olive oil and season to taste with salt and pepper.

To serve, place the bean purée in the middle of a serving platter and surround it with the shrimp. Garnish with arugula and drizzle with mint oil.

CANNELLINI BEAN PURÉE

½ cup plus 2 tablespoons extra virgin olive
   oil, divided

5 ounces pancetta, chopped

1 carrot, peeled and cut into large chunks

1 onion, cut into large chunks

1 stalk celery, cut into large chunks

2 cloves garlic

12 ounces dry cannellini beans, soaked in
   water overnight

6 cups vegetable stock

1 bouquet garni of 5 sage leaves, 5 sprigs
   thyme, and zest of 1 lemon

1 ounce rosemary, chopped

Salt and pepper, to taste

In a large stockpot, heat ¼ cup olive oil until hot. Add the pancetta and sauté briefly. Add the carrot, onion, celery, and garlic and cook until the vegetables are golden in color. Drain the beans from their water and add them to the vegetables. Add the vegetable stock and the bouquet garni. Bring to a boil, then lower the heat and simmer for 3 hours. Drain the mixture, pick the vegetables and bouquet garni from the beans and pass the beans through a food mill. Add the remaining olive oil and the chopped rosemary. Season to taste with salt and pepper.

TUSCAN SEAFOOD STEW

LISA SLAY AND RACHEL MOELLER,
REMY'S KITCHEN & WINE BAR

SERVES 6

- ½ cup olive oil
- ½ cup red onion, diced
- 5 cloves garlic, chopped
- 1 ½ pounds assorted fish, such as halibut, salmon, and mahi mahi, cut into pieces
- ½ pound squid tubes, cut into ¼-inch rings
- 8 medium shrimp, peeled and deveined
- 12 mussels
- Kosher salt, to taste
- Black pepper, to taste
- ½ cup white wine
- 3 cups spicy tomato broth (recipe follows)
- 1 cup vegetable stock
- Chopped parsley

In a large stock pot, heat the olive oil. Add the red onion and garlic and sauté until softened. Add the fish, squid, shrimp, and mussels and sauté briefly. Season with salt and pepper, then deglaze the pot with the wine.

Add the spicy tomato broth and the vegetable stock, cover the pot and simmer until all of the seafood is cooked, about 5 to 7 minutes.

To serve, ladle the stew into bowls and sprinkle each with parsley.

SPICY TOMATO BROTH

- 2 tablespoons olive oil
- 1 large yellow onion, chopped
- ½ red onion, sliced
- 6 large tomatoes, diced
- 1 tablespoon chopped garlic
- ½ teaspoon kosher salt
- ½ teaspoon black pepper
- ½ cup red wine
- 4 cups vegetable stock
- ½ teaspoon red chile flakes
- ¼ teaspoon cayenne pepper

In a large stock pot, heat the oil. Add the onions and tomatoes and sauté until the onions begin to brown. Add the garlic, salt and pepper, and sauté for 2 minutes.

Deglaze the pot with the red wine, then add the vegetable stock. Add the chile flakes and cayenne and simmer for 30 minutes.

Allow the broth to cool, then purée it in batches in a blender or food processor.

Smoked Pacific Sturgeon

and Butternut Squash, Dinosaur Kale, and Fresh Garbanzo Beans with Porchetta di Testa

KEVIN NASHAN, SIDNEY STREET CAFÉ

SERVES 4 TO 6

2 butternut squash, halved and seeded

2 tablespoons olive oil

8 tablespoons (1 stick) butter

1 tablespoon rice wine vinegar

1 tablespoon cream

1 pound kale, cleaned and stemmed

2 ounces porchetta di testa or favorite cured meat, thinly sliced

½ red onion, julienned

3 tablespoons minced garlic

½ cup white wine

2 tablespoons honey

2 tablespoons Crystal hot sauce

1 pound garbanzo beans, washed and cleaned

2 tablespoons each thyme, tarragon and chervil, roughly chopped

½ cup crème fraîche

4 to 6 6-ounce pieces cold-smoked sturgeon (recipe follows)

Preheat the oven to 400 degrees.

Place the squash in a shallow pan with enough water to cover the bottom of the pan and roast for 1 hour. Allow to cool slightly, then scrape the pulp into a blender or food processor. Add the olive oil, butter, vinegar, and cream and purée until smooth. Season to taste with salt and reserve.

Coat a large wide but fairly shallow pot with olive oil and slowly sauté the porchetta di testa. Add the onion and garlic and sauté until soft. Add kale, then deglaze the pan with the white wine. Stir in the honey and hot sauce and season to taste with salt. Reserve.

Bring a large pot of salted water to a boil. Blanch the vegetables, then remove them from the water and plunge them into a bowl of ice water to stop the cooking.

Combine the thyme, tarragon, chervil and crème fraîche and reserve.

Sauté the sturgeon and reheat the other components, except the crème fraîche.

To serve, place a small portion of the squash purée on the plate, then add the nettles mixture and the ferns. Top with the sturgeon and garnish with the crème fraîche.

SMOKED STURGEON CURE MIX

1 pound kosher salt

1 pound brown sugar

1 orange, zested

1 lemon, zested

1 lime, zested

1 tablespoon five spice

1 tablespoon Chimayo chile

2 tablespoons thyme

4 to 6 6-ounce pieces sturgeon

Combine all of the ingredients except the fish and coat the sturgeon with the mixture. Refrigerate for 1 hour. Then rise and air dry in the refrigerator. Using the necessary equipment, cold smoke for 1½ hours. However, the easier route is to buy the salmon online from New York at Murray's Sturgeon Shop (murrayssturgeon.com) or Barney Greengrass (barneygreengrass.com).

Sides

**JUSTIN HAIFLEY,
THE TRAVERN
KITCHEN & BAR**

**Where do you go for
pizza?** The Good Pie.

**Your favorite Sunday
dinner?** Anything I can eat
on the couch … It's usually
my day off.

**Your favorite restaurant
(aside from your own)?**
Cafe Napoli or Napoli 2.

One great cookiing tip?
Seasoning, fresh herbs,
fleur de sel, butter.

Tater Tot Casserole

JUSTIN HAIFLEY, THE TAVERN KITCHEN & BAR

SERVES 8 TO 10

2 pounds tater tots, baked until crispy according to package directions

1 cup diced white onion

½ cup chopped green onion, plus extra for garnish

2 16-ounce cans cheddar cheese sauce

2 cups shredded sharp cheddar cheese

1 tablespoon kosher salt

1 teaspoon fresh-cracked black pepper

Sour cream, for garnish

Bacon bits, for garnish

Preheat the oven to 350 degrees.

Mix all of the ingredients in a large bowl. Pour into a baking dish. Bake for 20 minutes or until golden brown. Garnish with sour cream, bacon bits, and green onion.

Roasted Brussels Sprouts with Pancetta

JIM FIALA, THE CROSSING, LILUMA, LILUMA'S SIDE DOOR, AND ACERO

SERVES 10

3 pounds Brussels
  sprouts

7 ounces pancetta, cut
  into small dice

3 tablespoons unsalted
  butter

Salt, to taste

Extra virgin olive oil

Liluma serves this dish as a small side or tossed with orecchiette pasta and Parmesan cheese.

Preheat the oven to 400 degrees.

Cut the bases off the Brussels sprouts and remove the outer leaves. Cut the sprouts into quarters.

Heat a heavy-bottomed skillet over medium heat. Add the pancetta and cook until lightly browned. Add the sprouts, butter, and salt. Sauté until the sprouts begin to brown, about 2 minutes.

Place the skillet in the oven and bake for 7 minutes or until the sprouts are brown on the outside and soft inside.

Transfer to a warm serving bowl and top with a drizzle of extra virgin olive oil.

season with salt and pepper. Roast for 20 to 25 minutes, carefully turning the squash about halfway through.

Remove the squash from the oven and reduce the heat to 350 degrees.

Using a muffin tin as a guide, cut the puff pastry sheets into squares slightly larger than the cups of the muffin tin. Push a puff pastry square into each of the cups of the muffin tin, then fill the cup with the roasted squash. Fold the excess puff pastry over the top of the squash to create a purse.

Bake for 8 to10 minutes or until the puff pastry is done. Allow to cool and serve at room temperature.

WORLD'S GREATEST MASHED POTATOES

ERIC KELLY, SCAPE AMERICAN BISTRO

SERVES 8

This is not the only version of mashed potatoes we serve at Scape American Bistro, but this is the recipe I use for all of my holidays.

    4 pounds Yukon Gold potatoes, peeled
    2 cups crème fraîche
    2 sticks unsalted butter, diced
    Kosher salt, to taste
    Fresh-cracked black pepper, to taste
    ½ cup heavy cream (optional)

Cut the peeled potatoes into 2-inch chunks (no smaller) and place into a large stockpot. Fill with water to cover the potatoes by 3 inches. Bring to a boil and cook for 10 to 12 minutes or until fork-tender.

Drain the potatoes, then return them to the pot and place over medium heat. Cook off the excess moisture for 2 to 3 minutes.

Position a food mill over a mixing bowl and place the potatoes, crème fraîche and diced butter into the basket of the food mill. Turn the handle to pass the ingredients through the grinder. Don't forget to scrape the potatoes from the backside of the food mill into the bowl.

Season to taste with salt and pepper, folding in the seasoning with a rubber spatula to mix evenly.

Every potato holds differently; if the potatoes are too stiff, bring the heavy cream to a simmer and whisk into the potatoes.

SUCCOTASH

JOHN STUHLMAN, ECLIPSE

SERVES 6

    3 slices bacon, diced
    1 tablespoon unsalted butter
    2 cups fresh corn kernels
    10 ounces frozen baby lima beans
    ½ cup small-diced red bell pepper
    1 bunch green onions, diced (keep the white
      and green parts separate)
    ¾ cup heavy cream
    ¼ cup water
    ½ teaspoon salt
    ½ teaspoon black pepper

Cook the bacon in a 10-inch skillet over low heat until crispy. Remove the bacon, leaving the fat in the skillet. Add the butter, corn, beans, bell pepper and white parts of the onion. Cook for 2 minutes, stirring frequently. Add the cream, water, salt and pepper and simmer for 10 minutes. Stir in the bacon and the green parts of the onion. Adjust the salt and pepper if needed and serve.

EGGPLANT PARMESAN

KEVIN TAYLOR, BISTRO 1130

SERVES 6

1 baby eggplant, cut into 6 circles
¾-inch thick

Olive oil

Sea salt

2 eggs

2 tablespoons milk

¾ cup flour

1 cup breadcrumbs

Tomato sauce

Mozzarella cheese, thin sliced or shredded

Fresh basil leaves

Preheat the oven to 350 degrees.

Brush the eggplant with a little olive oil and sprinkle with sea salt. Roast on a sheet tray for about 8 minutes.

Mix the eggs with the milk. Set up a breading station: First dredge the eggplant slices in the flour; shake off the excess. Dip into the egg wash and then coat with breadcrumbs.

Heat a touch of oil in a nonstick skillet. Add the breaded eggplant and fry until crisped on both sides. Transfer to an oven-proof baking dish, cover with your favorite tomato sauce and mozzarella cheese, and place in the oven until warmed through and the cheese is melted. Garnish with fresh basil leaves.

CORN PUDDING

CASSY VIRES, HOME WINE KITCHEN

SERVES 6

5 tablespoons unsalted butter

½ cup all-purpose flour

1 ½ teaspoons sugar

1 teaspoon salt

1 ¾ cups milk

3 large eggs

4 cups fresh corn kernels

Freshly ground pepper

Preheat the oven to 375 degrees.

In a medium saucepan, melt the butter and whisk in the flour, sugar and salt. Cook over moderately high heat for 1 minute. Gradually whisk in the milk and cook over medium heat until the sauce thickens, about 5 minutes.

In a medium bowl, beat the eggs. Add ½ cup of the hot milk mixture to the eggs, whisking constantly. Repeat with the remaining milk mixture, adding the hot liquid ½ cup at a time, until all of the milk mixture has been added to the eggs. Fold in the corn and season with pepper.

Butter a 9-inch cast-iron skillet and pour in the corn mixture. Bake for 30 minutes or until the pudding is cooked through.

ROMESCO SAUCE

STEVEN CARAVELLI, PI

YIELDS 1 QUART

20 roma tomatoes

8 red peppers

1 yellow onion

4 slices country bread, crust removed

¼ cup olive oil

6 cloves garlic, peeled and roughly chopped

1 teaspoon thyme leaves

1 teaspoon crushed red pepper

1 cup Marcona almonds

Salt and pepper, to taste

1 tablespoon Spanish paprika

¼ cup sherry vinegar

Preheat the oven to 425 degrees.

Chop the vegetables and the bread into large pieces. Toss with the olive oil, garlic, thyme, and crushed red pepper and place in a roasting pan. Roast until deeply caramelized.

Add the almonds 3 minutes before the mixture is ready.

When the mixture has finished roasting, season with salt, pepper, Spanish paprika, and sherry vinegar.

Allow to cool slightly and purée in the blender.

Serve with grilled fish or meats.

SALSA VERDE

STEVEN CARAVELLI, PI

YIELDS 3 CUPS

1 packed cup parsley leaves

1 packed cup basil leaves

1 packed cup mint leaves

½ cup capers, drained

4 oil-packed anchovy fillets

2 garlic cloves, chopped

1 tablespoon Dijon mustard

1 tablespoon sugar

1 lemon, juiced and zested

2 cups extra-virgin olive oil

Salt and freshly ground black pepper, to taste

In a food processor, combine the parsley with the basil, mint, capers, anchovies, garlic, mustard, sugar, lemon juice, and zest and process to a paste.

With the machine on, slowly pour in the olive oil. Season with salt and black pepper.

GOLDEN TOMATO HORSERADISH GRANITA

REX HALE, THREE SIXTY

YIELDS 2 GALLONS

At Three Sixty, we serve this granita in a 4-ounce ramekin as a condiment for the oysters on the half shell. However, it makes at great summertime accompaniment for chilled seafood, chicken, pork or beef. It may also be used as an intermezzo in a multicourse meal.

Berry-Basil Lemonade 148
Spiced Poached Pears, 138
Bread Pudding w. apple Sauce 134
Apple Cobbler 129
Salsa Verde 116
Eggplant Mozzarella 115
Risotto con Punte de Asparagi 110
Shrimp Saltimbocca 100
Creole Cakes 99
Linguini Mare e Monte 89
Rigatoni alla Norma 85
Pasta funghi 84
Cheese fondue classic 85
Braised Lamb Shanks 83

Polenta w. Sausage 72
Slo-roasted pork loin 68
Chicken Spiedini & Risotto 67
Creole Chicken Clemenceau 61
Beef Wellington 59
Spätzle 57
companion Beef Stew 56
arugula Salad 52
Potato Salad, German 47
arugula Salad 45
Spinach Salad 44
Tomato Bisque 38
Two Bean Soup 39
Brie LT 29
Bruschetta di Pompadora 20
artichoke Hearts w. Lemon Aioi 11

5 pounds ripe golden tomatoes

5 yellow peppers

½ cup dry sherry

½ cup plus 2 tablespoons sherry vinegar

½ cup plus 2 tablespoons extra virgin olive oil

5 tablespoons sugar

Sea salt and freshly ground black pepper,
    to taste

¾ cup minced shallots

1 cup freshly grated horseradish root

Chop the tomatoes and yellow peppers and place them in the bowl of a food processor. Purée until smooth. Add the dry sherry, sherry vinegar, olive oil, sugar and a pinch of salt and process until combined.

Strain the mixture through a fine-mesh strainer into a bowl. Add the shallots and horseradish. Pour the mixture into an 8- or 9-inch nonreactive baking dish and freeze until partially frozen, about 1 hour. Scrape and stir with a fork, crushing any lumps. Continue to freeze, scraping once or twice, until evenly frozen, about 2 more hours.

GOLDEN RAISIN MOSTARDA

JOHN GRIFFITHS

YIELDS 2 CUPS

This Italian condiment complements roasted or grilled meats and aged cheeses.

8 ounces golden raisins, soaked in warm water

1 cup pistachios

3 tablespoons braised mustard seeds
    (recipe follows)

½ cup white balsamic vinegar

2 tablespoons honey

3 tablespoons olive oil

Cover mustard seeds with water and simmer for 15 minutes, then cover and steep for 15 minutes. Refrigerate. They'll be good for two weeks.

Combine all of the ingredients except the olive oil in a saucepan and cook over medium heat until the vinegar reduces by three-quarters and begins to thicken. Add the olive oil and season with salt. Cool and reserve for up to one week.

Serve with roasted meats, grilled sausages, and even cheeses.

BACON JAM

JUSTIN HAIFLEY,
THE TAVERN KITCHEN & BAR

YIELDS 1 QUART

3 pounds bacon, cut into 2-inch pieces

2 tablespoons chopped garlic

1 red onion, large diced

2 cups ruby port wine

½ cup brown sugar

1 tablespoon fresh thyme leaves

2 bay leaves

2 tablespoons fresh cracked black pepper

Sauté bacon in a skillet until crispy. Add garlic and onion and sauté for 4 minutes. Add port wine, brown sugar, thyme, bay leaves, and black pepper. Cook over medium-high heat until port wine is reduced by three-fourths.

Process the mixture in a food processer until finely puréed. Cool and store in the refrigerator.

SWEET CORN SUCCOTASH SAUCE

DON TADLOCK, KEMOLL'S

SERVES 6 TO 8

Serve this sauce with chicken, fish, beef, pork—it's even perfect over potatoes.

6 to 8 large ears of corn, shucked

½ to 1 cup honey

Salt and pepper, to taste

1 cup white wine

4 sticks butter, divided

1 red onion, finely diced

1 leek, finely diced

½ cup pancetta or bacon, finely diced

1 cup prosciutto, finely diced

1 red bell pepper, finely diced

½ poblano pepper, finely diced

2 to 3 tablespoons garlic, finely diced

2 cups chicken stock

1 quart 40-percent heavy cream

1 teaspoon sweet basil, fresh

1 teaspoon oregano, fresh

1 teaspoon paprika

1 tablespoon salt

1 tablespoon black pepper

1 tablespoon garlic powder

1 teaspoon chopped parsley

Coat a rimmed baking sheet with cooking spray. Preheat the oven to 350 degrees.

Cut the kernels from the corn into a bowl. Add the honey and toss to coat. Spread the kernels onto the baking sheet evenly. Season to taste with salt and pepper.

Roast the corn for 10 to 15 minutes. Remove from the oven and deglaze with the white wine. Set aside.

In a medium-sized pot, melt two sticks of butter over medium-low heat. Add the red onions, leeks, pancetta, and prosciutto. Once you see slight color, add the red bell peppers, poblano, garlic, and corn. Stir for 1 to 2 minutes and then deglaze with chicken stock. Bring to a simmer and allow the sauce to reduce for 3 to 4 minutes.

Bring to a boil, then reduce the heat to low. Slowly temper in the heavy cream. Add herbs and spices, remove from the heat and stir in the remaining two sticks of butter. Stir in the parsley.

PARMESAN PULL-APARTS

JUSTIN HAIFLEY, THE TAVERN KITCHEN & BAR

SERVES 6

¼ cup (½ stick) butter

2 teaspoons minced parsley

¼ teaspoon celery seed

¼ teaspoon minced garlic

¼ teaspoon dried chili flakes

1 teaspoon chopped fresh thyme

¼ teaspoon dried oregano

1 package refrigerated biscuits

¼ cup grated Parmesan cheese

Preheat the oven to 425 degrees.

Melt the butter in an 8-inch cake pan. Add the seasonings.

Cut the biscuits into quarters. Place them on top of the butter and seasonings. Pack them in snugly. Sprinkle liberally with Parmesan cheese.

Bake for 10 to 14 minutes.

CORN BREAD

ERIC KELLY, SCAPE AMERICAN BISTRO

SERVES 12

- 1 cup yellow cornmeal
- 1 cup all-purpose flour
- ⅓ cup cake flour
- 1 cup granulated sugar
- 2 tablespoons baking powder
- 1 tablespoon iodized salt
- 8 ½ tablespoons butter, divided
- ¼ cup plus 1 tablespoon vegetable oil
- 4 large eggs, lightly beaten
- 1 cup whole milk
- ½ cup buttermilk
- ¼ cup honey
- ⅓ cup water

Preheat the oven to 350 degrees. Coat a 9-by-13-inch baking dish with cooking spray. Sift together the dry ingredients and set aside.

Melt 2 ½ tablespoons of butter and mix it with the vegetable oil. Allow to cool slightly, then whisk the mixture into the eggs. Combine both milks, then whisk them into the egg mixture. Whisk the dry ingredients into the egg mixture. Using a rubber spatula, scrape the batter into the prepared baking dish. Bake for 20 to 25 minutes, turn the pan and bake another 10 minutes or until a toothpick inserted in the center comes out clean. Remove from the oven and cool on a rack for 10 minutes.

Using a wooden skewer, poke holes in the surface of the bread every half-inch, going all the way to the bottom of the pan. Combine the remaining 6 tablespoons of butter, the honey, and water in a small saucepan and bring to a boil. Remove from the heat. Using a pastry brush, brush the honey-butter over the bread. Cut the bread into squares and serve.

RUSTIC PASTA DOUGH

VITO RACCANELLI, MAD TOMATO

SERVES MANY

- 2 pounds "00" flour
- 1 ½ cups plus 2 tablespoons water

Mix the flour and water for 30 minutes in stand mixer fitted with a dough hook.

Portion out into 6- to 8-ounce balls. Wrap each ball in plastic wrap and let sit for 1 hour before rolling.

Using a pasta maker or a rolling pin, roll the dough out to your desired thickness and cut into desired shapes. Cook in a pot of salted boiling water until al dente.

VITO RACANNELLI, MAD TOMATO

What is the one ingredient pantries should always have? Really good olive oil from Italy.

Where do you go for pizza? Racanelli's New York Pizza in the Central West End.

Is there one dish you just never get right? My mother's meatballs.

What appliance do you use the most? I love my Vitamix Blender.

Focaccia
(Mad Tomato Table Bread)

VITO RACANNELLI, MAD TOMATO

SERVES 10

- 3 cups very cold water
- 3 teaspoons dry Instant yeast
- 2 teaspoons sugar
- 5 teaspoons sea salt, divided
- 1 cup plus 2 tablespoons olive oil, divided
- 2 ½ pounds high-gluten bread flour
- 1 cup crushed whole peeled tomatoes
- 1 teaspoon oregano
- 1 teaspoon sea salt

In a stand mixer fitted with a dough hook, combine the water, yeast, and sugar and mix for 8 minutes. Add 4 teaspoons of the salt and ½ cup plus 2 tablespoons of the olive oil and mix for 4 more minutes.

Add the flour and mix for 12 to 15 minutes, or until the dough comes off the bowl. Roll the dough into a large ball and place on an oiled half-sheet pan. Cover it loosely with plastic wrap and refrigerate for 8 hours.

Remove from the refrigerator. Flatten the dough on a sheet pan, brushing ½ cup of olive oil evenly on the top and bottom. Place the crushed tomatoes on top and spread evenly, pushing the tomatoes into the dough with your fingertips. Sprinkle the oregano and the remaining 1 teaspoon salt on top.

Preheat the oven to 350 degrees.

Let the focaccia rise at room temperature for 1 hour. Bake for 25 minutes.

Desserts

BLUEBERRY BREAD PUDDIN'

TONY ALMOND,
ALMONDS RESTAURANT

SERVES 6

8 vanilla egg buns*

4 pints fresh blueberries (or other fresh fruit)

8 large eggs

3 cups sugar

1 quart 40-percent cream

Dash salt

2 tablespoons vanilla extract

Caramel sauce or ice cream

Preheat the oven to 425 degrees.

Cut the buns into 1-inch cubes. Place half of the cubed bread in the bottom of a 9-by-12-by-3-inch baking dish. Evenly spread half of the blueberries over this layer. Place the remaining bread on top, then cover it with the remaining blueberries. Set aside.

Crack the eggs into a mixing bowl and add the sugar. Beat for about 30 to 45 seconds or until the sugar dissolves. Set aside.

In a 4-quart saucepan, heat the cream to a simmer. Be careful not to allow it to boil. Slowly add the cream to the egg mixture while whipping with a wire whisk. It is important to add the hot cream to the eggs slowly, to prevent the eggs from scrambling. Add a dash of salt and 2 tablespoons of vanilla extract.

Pour the mixture evenly over the pan of bread and blueberries. Bake for 15 minutes on the center rack. Reduce the heat to 350 degrees and cook for 1 hour or until the top is golden brown.

Serve warm with caramel sauce and/or ice cream.

* Available at Breadsmith

ORANGES MACERATED IN COGNAC AND HONEY

TIM BRENNAN, CRAVINGS

SERVES 6 TO 8

8 navel oranges, unpeeled, preferably bright orange and seedless

½ cup honey, preferably local and mild-tasting

1 cup good-quality Cognac

Seeds from 1 large pomegranate

Leaving the rind on, cut the oranges into ¼-inch slices.

Gently warm the honey in the microwave. Stir in the cognac and pour the mixture over the oranges. Refrigerate for 4 to 6 hours or until the flavors blend together.

Sprinkle pomegranate seeds on top just before serving.

GRAMMA BUDDE'S HOT MILK SPONGE CAKE

BETHANY BUDDE-COHEN, SQWIRES

YIELDS 1 SHEET PAN

This great family cake recipe is on SqWires' menu all summer long. It's served with homegrown berries or sliced fruit and fresh whipped cream.

6 eggs

3 cups sugar

3 cups sifted flour

3 tablespoons baking powder

1 ½ teaspoons salt

1 ½ cups milk

10 ½ tablespoons butter

1 ½ teaspoons vanilla extract

Fresh berries or sliced fruit

Whipped cream

12 tablespoons (1 ½ sticks) unsalted butter, cold and diced small

2 ¼ cups sugar

3 eggs, separated

½ cup buttermilk

3 ounces semi-sweet chocolate, grated

½ teaspoon cream of tartar

Preheat the oven to 300 degrees. Grease and flour a sheet pan.

Beat the eggs with a hand mixer on high speed. Gradually add the sugar until it turns a lemony color. Fold in the sifted flour, baking powder, and salt.

Bring the milk and butter to a boil and add it to the flour mixture. Add the vanilla extract and stir by hand until smooth. Pour into the prepared sheet pan and bake for 20 minutes. Check every 7 to 10 minutes. The cake is done when the center springs back to the touch.

Cool completely. If not using immediately, store and cover at room temperature. Cut into squares or disks. Layer with fruit and fresh whipped cream.

VERMONT CHOCOLATE POTATO CAKE

BILL CARDWELL, CARDWELL'S AT THE PLAZA AND BC'S KITCHEN

SERVES 8 TO 10

2 baked russet potatoes

1 ¾ cups cake flour, sifted

2 teaspoons baking powder

1 teaspoon salt

½ teaspoon ground clove

½ teaspoon ground cinnamon

½ teaspoon ground nutmeg

½ teaspoon ground ginger

Preheat the oven to 350 degrees. Butter and flour a tube pan.

Peel the potatoes and put through a potato ricer. Reserve 1 cup.

Sift together the cake flour, baking powder, salt, and spices.

In a stand mixer, cream together the butter and sugar until light and fluffy. Add the egg yolks one at a time, blending well after each addition. Add the reserved riced potato. Alternate adding portions of the dry ingredients and the buttermilk, finishing with flour. Add the chocolate.

Whip together the egg whites and cream of tartar until firm, then fold into the batter.

Pour the batter into the prepared pan. Bake until set, approximately 1 hour. Cool and unmold. Serve with whipped cream and chocolate sauce.

STILTON BLUE CHEESE ICE CREAM WITH BLACK TRUFFLE HONEY AND FRIED SALT-CURED BACON

ANTHONY DEVOTI, FIVE BISTRO

SERVES 4 TO 6

4 ounces Stilton blue cheese

6 tablespoons honey

4 thin slices salt-cured bacon

½ cup whole milk

2 cups heavy cream

4 egg yolks

¼ cup sugar

Black truffle honey

Blend together the cheese and honey until smooth. Set aside.

Fry the bacon until crisp. Drain on paper towels and crumble when cool.

In a saucepan, bring the milk and cream to a boil. In a bowl, whisk together the egg yolks and sugar. Temper the eggs by adding ½ cup of the hot cream to the eggs. Pour the tempered eggs into the hot cream mixture and cook, stirring, over low heat until thickened slightly and the mixture coats the back of a spoon.

Remove the pan from the heat and slowly whisk in the cheese mixture. Strain through a fine-mesh sieve, chill and then process in an ice cream maker.

Scoop the ice cream into serving dishes and drizzle with the truffle honey. Top with the bacon.

BITTERSWEET CHOCOLATE TORTE

MARC FELIX, CONSULTING CHEF

SERVES 12

3 ⅔ cups all-purpose flour

2 ½ sticks plus 1 ½ tablespoons butter

¾ cup sugar

2 egg yolks

Ice water

1 pound bittersweet Valrhona chocolate*, chipped

2 whole eggs

1 ⅔ cups heavy cream

1 cup milk

Mix the flour and sugar together, then add the butter and yolks and blend together with pastry cutter. If the crust looks dry, then add ice water, a little at a time. Shape into a disc, wrap in plastic, and chill.

Place the chocolate in the top of a double boiler. As it melts, blend in the milk and cream. Pour the mixture into a medium bowl and add the eggs. Mix together. Let the filling cool.

Preheat the oven to 350 degrees. Roll out the dough to ¼-inch thickness and press into the bottom of two 9-inch tart pans. Place the tart pans on a half-sheet pan and pour the filling into the crusts to just below the rim.

Bake for 35 minutes or until the center is set.

Available at cocosphere.com

APPLE COBBLER

JIM FIALA, THE CROSSING, LILUMA, LILUMA'S SIDE DOOR, AND ACERO

SERVES 15 TO 20

1 cup milk

2 cups all-purpose flour, divided

½ cup white granulated sugar, plus extra for dusting

10 apples, peeled and sliced ¼-inch thick

1 teaspoon cinnamon

½ cup brown sugar

Pinch salt

4 sticks butter, very cold and cut into pieces

Preheat the oven to 350 degrees.

Mix together the milk, 1 cup of the flour, and the granulated sugar. Set aside.

Butter a 9-by-13-inch baking dish, dust with sugar, and then fill the bottom of the dish with the milk mixture. Pour the apples on top of the mixture and sprinkle with the cinnamon.

In a separate bowl, combine the remaining 1 cup flour, with the brown sugar and salt. Using your hands, work the cold butter into the dry mixture. (The butter should be very cold—this is what makes the topping crisp.) Continue to work the butter into the dry ingredients until the mixture is sandy in texture. Do not overwork; it should be a rough, meal consistency, not pasty.

Crumble the topping over the apple dish and bake for 45 minutes.

CHOCOLATE-GRAND MARNIER CRÈME CARAMEL

BRIAN S. HALE

SERVES 6

6 egg yolks

1 ½ cups sugar, divided

1 vanilla bean, split lengthwise

2 cups heavy cream

4 ounces semisweet chocolate

1 tablespoon Grand Marnier

1 tablespoon water

6 mint leaves

12 raspberries

Preheat the oven to 325 degrees.

Combine the egg yolks and ½ cup sugar in a stainless steel bowl and whisk until the mixture is creamy. Combine the vanilla bean and cream in a pot and heat to a boil. Remove from the heat and scrape the pulp from the vanilla bean into the cream. Discard the bean and reserve the mixture.

Using a double boiler, melt the chocolate. Add the chocolate and the Grand Marnier to the cream mixture. Slowly pour the chocolate mixture into the egg mixture while constantly stirring. Place the remaining 1 cup sugar and the water into a heavy-bottomed skillet and cook until the mixture is smooth and a deep amber color. Stir the mixture constantly to avoid burning. Spoon enough of this caramel into 6 ramekins to cover the bottom of each. Let cool for 5 minutes. Pour the custard into the ramekins and place them in a baking dish filled with about an inch of water. Bake for 2 hours. Cool to room temperature, then refrigerate overnight. To serve, run a paring knife around the inside of the ramekin and tap the custard out onto a serving plate. Garnish with fresh mint and raspberries.

Top of the Hill Farm Blackberry Crisp

LOU ROOK III, ANNIE GUNN'S

SERVES 6

½ cup all-purpose flour

½ cup sugar

1 ½ teaspoons baking powder

6 tablespoons melted butter

2 pounds or 2 quarts blackberries

½ cup vanilla sugar

¼ cup honey

Zest of 1 lemon

½ teaspoon kosher salt

Four twists of the peppermill

¼ teaspoon ground cinnamon

Vanilla bean ice cream

Preheat the oven to 350 degrees.

Combine the flour, sugar, baking powder, and butter and mix with a fork or a dough hook until well combined. Allow to rest for 15 minutes.

Combine the berries, vanilla sugar, honey, lemon zest, salt, pepper, and cinnamon and mix together until juices start forming. Fill six 8-ounce ramekins with the berry mixture. Top each with the crisp mixture.

Bake for 15 to 20 minutes. Serve with a scoop of vanilla bean ice cream.

ZABAGLIONE WITH FRESH BERRIES

RICH LORUSSO, LORUSSO'S CUCINA

SERVES 4

6 egg yolks

1 egg white

⅓ cup granulated sugar

¼ cup sweet Marsala wine

Fresh berries

Combine all of the ingredients except the berries and whisk until blended. Cook in a double boiler very slowly, constantly beating with a wire whisk for about 5 minutes or until the custard is very light in color and resembles soft whipped cream. Be careful not to scramble the egg; pull the saucepan off the heat if it seems to be congealing too quickly.

Remove from the heat and pour into dessert cups. Top with fresh berries of your choice.

CRÈME BRÛLÉE WITH STRAWBERRIES

CARL McCONNELL, STONE SOUP COTTAGE

SERVES 4

5 egg yolks

1 whole egg

¾ cup sugar, plus ¼ cup for dusting

Pinch salt

¼ teaspoon vanilla extract

2 cups heavy cream, heated

8 fresh strawberries, stemmed and halved

Drizzle of lavender honey

Preheat the oven to 350 degrees.

Whisk together the egg yolks, whole egg, ¾ cup sugar, salt, and vanilla extract in a stainless steel bowl. Temper the eggs by vigorously whisking 2 tablespoons of the hot cream into the egg mixture. Add the remaining cream and stir well. Skim the accumulated foam off the top of the custard with a spoon. Evenly distribute the custard base into 4 ramekins. Place the ramekins in a roasting pan and fill the roasting pan with very hot water to a level halfway up the side of the ramekins. Bake for 20 to 30 minutes or until the custards are firm. Refrigerate the custards for at least 3 hours. Dust the tops of the chilled custards with sugar. Shake off excess sugar. Using a crème brûlée torch, flambé the sugared tops until caramelized.

In a bowl, toss the strawberries with lavender honey. Serve the berries with the crème brûlée.

MIXED BERRY PIE

CARY McDOWELL, WINSLOW'S HOME

SERVES 8

5 cups mixed berries (blueberries, blackberries, and raspberries when possible, though any combination works)

¾ cup sugar

¼ cup flour

¼ teaspoon cinnamon

1 teaspoon lemon juice

2 9-inch pie crusts, unbaked

2 tablespoons butter

Preheat the oven to 350 degrees.

Gently mix the berries in bowl with the sugar, flour, cinnamon, and lemon juice.

Roll out one of the crusts and place it in a pie pan, leaving about ¾ inch hanging over edge. Pour the berries into the dough-lined pie pan. Cut the butter into small pieces, and dot them on top of the berries.

Roll out the second crust, and cut several decorative slits in it. Then place the crust over the berries in the pie pan, again leaving about ¾ inch of dough hanging over the edge. Fold the top dough over bottom dough, tucking both under together, and press the fold against the pie pan's edge. Flute the crust's edge with your fingers.

Bake for 45 to 60 minutes or until the crust is golden and berry juice bubbles up through the slits.

WARMED BRIOCHE BREAD PUDDING WITH BOURBON-CURRANT SAUCE AND VANILLA WHIPPED CREAM

NICK MILLER, HARVEST

SERVES 12

2 cups milk

4 cups heavy cream, divided

2 ¾ cups plus 2 tablespoons granulated sugar, divided

1 ¾ teaspoons vanilla extract, divided

½ vanilla bean

½ cinnamon stick

¼ teaspoon freshly ground nutmeg

3 whole eggs

3 egg yolks

2 loaves brioche, crusts removed and cut into ½-inch cubes

½ teaspoon baking soda

2 tablespoons light corn syrup

1 cup buttermilk 2 sticks unsalted butter

½ cup bourbon

½ cup dried currants

12 mint sprigs

Powdered sugar

Preheat the oven to 350 degrees.

In a saucepot, combine the milk, 2 cups of the cream, ¾ cup of the sugar, ¼ teaspoon of the vanilla extract, the vanilla bean, cinnamon, and nutmeg. Bring the mixture to a boil and remove from the heat. Discard the vanilla bean and the cinnamon stick.

In a mixing bowl, whisk together the eggs and egg yolks. Slowly pour half the hot cream mixture into the eggs and whisk to incorporate. Add the remaining cream mixture and whisk together. Let the custard cool slightly.

Place the brioche in a mixing bowl and pour in the custard. Toss the ingredients together lightly and place in a buttered or greased 9-by-13-inch baking dish. Bake approximately 25 to 30 minutes or until the top is a golden brown.

Meanwhile, combine 2 cups sugar, baking soda, ½ teaspoon vanilla extract, corn syrup, buttermilk, and butter in a saucepot and bring to a boil. Remove from the heat, add the bourbon and currants, and set aside.

In a mixer, combine the remaining 2 cups heavy cream, 2 tablespoons sugar, and 1 teaspoon vanilla extract. Whip until stiff peaks form.

Remove the bread pudding from the oven. Cut into desired sized pieces and serve in a dessert bowl topped with the bourbon-currant sauce and a dollop of whipped cream. Garnish with a sprig of mint and a dusting of powdered sugar.

TIRAMISU

ZOE ROBINSON, I FRATELLINI AND BOBO NOODLE HOUSE

SERVES 12

1 ½ pounds mascarpone cheese

1 ½ cups sugar

2 egg yolks

1 teaspoon vanilla

4 cups whipped cream, divided

4 cups strong coffee

3 teaspoons Marsala wine

2 teaspoons Kahlúa

48 lady fingers

Cocoa for dusting

In a large mixing bowl, combine the mascarpone, sugar, eggs, vanilla, and three of the cups of whipped cream.

In a separate bowl, combine the coffee, Marsala, and Kahlúa.

Line a rectangular casserole dish with 24 lady fingers and soak with half of the coffee mixture. Top with half of the mascarpone mixture. Layer the remaining lady fingers and repeat. Top with the remaining cup of whipped cream and dust with cocoa powder.

Cover and refrigerate until ready to serve.

BREAD PUDDING WITH APPLE BUTTER

TOM SUTCLIFFE, PRIME 1000

SERVES 12

2 cups heavy cream

2 cups milk

3 egg yolks

3 whole eggs

1 cup sugar

1 tablespoon vanilla extract

2 loaves day-old Italian bread, cut into 2-inch cubes

Apple butter (recipe follows)

Tahitian vanilla bean ice cream

Combine the cream and milk in a saucepan and bring to a boil. Remove from the heat.

Whisk together the eggs, sugar and vanilla in a large mixing bowl. Slowly whisk the hot cream mixture into the egg mixture. Chill for 1 hour. Once chilled, combine the custard with the bread.

Preheat the oven to 325 degrees. Butter a 9-by-13-inch casserole dish. Place the bread pudding into the dish and bake on the center rack for 30 minutes.

Place a spoonful of apple butter on chilled plates. Top with a slice of warm bread pudding and serve with a scoop of Tahitian vanilla bean ice cream.

APPLE BUTTER

6 Granny Smith apples, cored and quartered

2 cups apple cider

2 cups sugar

2 cloves

2 teaspoons allspice

2 tablespoons cinnamon

1 teaspoon nutmeg

Combine all of the ingredients in a large saucepot and cook over low heat until the apples are soft.

Position a food mill over a bowl and place the apple mixture in the bowl of the mill. Pass the mixture through the mill, then return it to the pan and cook over low heat for 2 to 3 hours or until thick.

Allow to cool, then refrigerate until chilled.

WARM CHOCOLATE CAKE

TED WATT,
THE GARDENS AT MALMAISON

SERVES 8

1 ½ cups finely chopped semisweet chocolate

3 tablespoons unsalted butter

2 ½ egg yolks

¼ cup almond flour

1 tablespoon cornstarch

1 tablespoon cocoa powder

7 egg whites

½ cup granulated sugar

Preheat the oven to 350 degrees. Butter eight 4-inch ramekins.

In a double boiler over hot water, melt the chocolate and butter.

Using an electric mixer, whisk the egg yolks until pale and foamy. Fold in the melted chocolate, then fold in the almond flour, cornstarch, and cocoa powder.

Whisk the egg whites until soft peaks form, then add the sugar and continue to whisk for 1 minute. Fold the whites into the batter.

Pour the batter into the ramekins and bake until set firm, about 15 minutes.

The cakes should rise during baking and then fall once out of the oven. Remove from oven and allow to cool slightly, then tip out of the ramekins onto serving plates.

CRÈME CARAMEL

TED WATT,
THE GARDENS AT MALMAISON

SERVES 8

2 ½ cups granulated sugar

2 cups water, divided

2 cups milk

1 vanilla bean

1 cinnamon stick

½ cardamom pod

3 whole eggs

2 egg yolks

In a heavy saucepan, combine 2 cups sugar and 1 cup water. Boil until deep amber, stirring frequently to prevent burning. Pour the mixture into a 5-by-9-inch loaf pan, coating it with the hot caramel. Allow to cool.

Combine the milk, vanilla bean, cinnamon, cardamom, and remaining ½ cup sugar in a saucepan and bring to a simmer. Remove from the heat and let the liquid steep for 20 minutes, then cool in an ice bath. Discard the vanilla bean.

Preheat the oven to 300 degrees. Once the milk mixture is cooled, add the eggs and yolks, whisking to combine. Pass through a fine sieve and pour the custard into the caramel-lined loaf pan. Set the pan in a hot water bath, using the remaining 1 cup of water, and bake until firm, about 45 minutes. Allow to cool, then refrigerate overnight.

To serve, carefully remove the crème caramel from the pan and cut to desired size.

CASSY VIRES, HOME WINE KITCHEN

Your favorite kitchen tool? A good, sharp knife that fits perfectly to my hand.

One great cooking tip? Keep it simple. Sometimes the best food is the simplest techniques just done really well to quality ingredients.

Your favorite five-ingredient dish? Ice cream. Eggs, sugar, milk, cream, and flavoring. So simple, yet so satisfying.

Lemon Pudding Soufflé

CASSY VIRES, HOME WINE KITCHEN

SERVES 8

4 tablespoons unsalted butter, melted and cooled slightly

1 cup granulated sugar, divided

3 large eggs, separated, at room temperature

1 ⅛ ounces all-purpose flour

⅛ teaspoon table salt

1 ¼ cups milk, at room temperature

⅓ cup lemon juice, at room temperature

1 tablespoon finely grated lemon zest

Position a rack in the center of the oven and heat the oven to 350 degrees. Butter eight 6-ounce ceramic oven-proof ramekins and arrange them in a baking dish filled with warm water.

In a large bowl, whisk the melted butter with ⅔ cup of the sugar and the egg yolks until smooth and light, about 1 minute. Add the flour and salt and pour in just enough milk to whisk the flour smoothly into the egg yolk mixture. Then whisk in the remaining milk and the lemon juice until smooth.

Put the egg whites in a large bowl. Beat with an electric mixer on medium speed until the whites form soft peaks. Reduce the mixer speed to medium, and with the mixer running, very slowly sprinkle in the remaining ⅓ cup sugar, scraping the sides of the bowl. Beat on high speed until the whites hold medium-firm peaks when the beater is pulled away.

Scrape one-third of the egg whites into the egg yolk mixture, sprinkle the lemon zest on top, and whisk until combined. Gently incorporate the remaining whites into the batter, using the whisk in a folding, stirring motion.

Portion the mixture evenly among the ramekins. Bake until the tops of the cakes are lightly golden, slightly puffed and, when touched with a finger, spring back a bit but hold a shallow indentation, 25 to 30 minutes. Transfer the ramekins to a rack and cool to room temperature.

Refrigerate for at least 2 hours and up to 24 hours before serving.

SPICED POACHED PEARS

TED WATT,
THE GARDENS AT MALMAISON

SERVES 4

4 Anjou pears

1 cup granulated sugar

2 cups water

Juice of 1 lemon

Juice of 1 orange

1 cardamom pod

½ vanilla bean

1 cinnamon stick

½ fresh bay leaf

10 white peppercorns

Peel, core, and halve the pears. Combine the pears and the remaining ingredients in a saucepan. Bring to a low boil, reduce the heat, and simmer until tender, about 15 minutes. Place the pears and liquid in an ice bath to cool.

To serve, place the pears on four serving plates and spoon the cooking liquid over the top.

PEACH-CHERRY COBBLER CRISP

BETH WILLIAMS, TABLE THREE

SERVES 10 TO 12

6 tablespoons butter

4 cups peaches, peeled and sliced

1 cup sugar

1 cup brown sugar

1 ½ cups Bing cherries, pitted

¼ cup amaretto liqueur

Pinch salt

¼ teaspoon cinnamon

Cobbler Crisp topping (recipe follows)

Preheat the oven to 350 degrees.

In a large saucepot, melt the butter over medium-high heat. Add the peaches and sugars and cook for approximately 8 minutes or until almost tender. Increase the heat, and add the cherries, amaretto, salt, and cinnamon. Stir and remove from the heat. Transfer the fruit mixture to a large baking dish. Top with cobbler topping and bake for 12 to 15 minutes or until topping is golden brown. Serve warm with vanilla ice cream.

COBBLER CRISP TOPPING

10 tablespoons butter, divided and at room temperature

¼ cup chopped hazelnuts, toasted

½ cup brown sugar

½ cup sugar

1 ¾ cup plus 1 tablespoon flour, divided

4 teaspoons baking powder

¼ teaspoon salt

4 ounces white chocolate chips or chopped white chocolate bark (optional)

¼ cup milk

Preheat the oven to 350 degrees.

Melt 4 tablespoons of butter and combine it in a bowl with the hazelnuts, sugars, and 1 tablespoon flour. Bake for 5 to 10 minutes or until golden brown. Let cool completely.

In a food processor or bowl, combine the remaining 1¾ cups flour, baking powder, and salt. Blend thoroughly. Add the cooled hazelnut mixture, then cut in the remaining 6 tablespoons butter and the white chocolate, if using, until the mixture is crumbly. Add the milk and pulse until it is fully incorporated. Be careful not to overmix.

Drinks

THE VENETIAN

BROOKSEY CARDWELL, BC'S KITCHEN

SERVES 1

1 egg white

1 ½ ounces Bombay Gin

1 ounce Aperol

½ ounce fresh orange juice

½ ounce fresh lime juice

½ ounce pomegranate molasses or
pomegranate grenadine

Orange twist

Place the egg white in a cocktail shaker and shake until frothy, no more than 10 seconds.

Add ice to the shaker, then add the gin, Aperol, orange juice, lime juice, and grenadine. Shake until combined and chilled. Strain into a martini glass and garnish with orange twist.

NOUVEAU MOJITO

BROOKSEY CARDWELL, BC'S KITCHEN

SERVES 1

2 ounces mint-infused rum*

2 ounces fresh grapefruit juice

1 ounce mint syrup**

1 ounce club soda

Mint sprig

Fresh sugar cane

Combine the rum, grapefruit juice, and syrup in a cocktail shaker and shake to combine. Fill a Collins glass with cracked ice. Add the rum mixture and top with club soda. Garnish with a mint sprig and fresh sugar cane.

To make the mint-infused rum, pour 1 bottle of high-quality white rum over 30 fresh-picked mint leaves. Add the zest of one lime and leave in a glass container for one week, shaking once every day. Strain and use.

**To make mint syrup, combine 1 cup of sugar and 1 cup of water in a pan and bring to a boil. Turn off the heat, add 30 fresh mint leaves and steep for 20 minutes. Strain—or, for a stronger mint flavor, blend then strain—through cheesecloth. Store in the refrigerator for up to two weeks.*

THE VELVET EDIE:
A PLAY ON ANDY
WARHOL'S FAVORITE
COCKTAIL

JUSTIN CARDWELL, BC'S KITCHEN

SERVES 1

7 raspberries, plus extra for garnish

3 fresh mint leaves

2 lemon wedges

3 ounces Dolin Blanco Sweet Vermouth

Lemon twist

Muddle the raspberries, mint, and lemon wedges in a shaker. Top with ice and vermouth. Shake until combined and chilled. Double-strain into a chilled martini glass. Garnish with fresh raspberries and lemon twist.

LYCHEE BELLINI

MARC FELIX, CONSULTING CHEF

SERVES 6

- 1 can lychees in syrup*
- ⅛ teaspoon grenadine
- 1 bottle Prosecco

Pour lychees, syrup, and grenadine into a blender and purée. Strain through a sieve, using the back of a ladle to help push the liquid through. Divide the purée between six champagne flutes, then top off with the Prosecco.

Available at Global Market

BOURBON BLOSSOM

JAMIE KILGORE, NICHE

SERVES 1

- 2 ounces Four Roses bourbon
- ¾ ounce St. Germain Elderflower liqueur
- ½ ounce Cointreau
- ½ ounce orange juice
- Orange twist

Combine all of the ingredients except the orange twist in a shaker filled with ice. Shake vigorously, then strain into a chilled cocktail glass. Garnish with an orange twist.

THE MR. SMITH

STEVEN FITZPATRICK SMITH, THE ROYALE FOOD & SPIRITS

SERVES 1

- 1 ½ ounces dry gin
- ½ ounce mint simple syrup
- ½ ounce fresh lime juice
- Ginger beer (recommended: Schlafly Osterweis)
- Lime wedge

Combine the gin, mint simple syrup, and lime juice in a cocktail shaker. Shake until combined, then strain into a 12-ounce, ice-filled glass. Top with the ginger beer. Garnish with a lime wedge.

MAI TAI, BABY

TED KILGORE, TASTE

SERVES 1

- 1 ounce Angostura 5 year rum
- 1 ounce Rhum Barbancourt (Haitian rum)
- ½ ounce My Amaro (herbal liqueur)
- ½ ounce Orgeat
- ¾ ounce lime juice
- 6 dashes Angostura bitters (float)

Shake and strain all but Ango into highball glass with pebble ice. Top with Angostura bitters. Garnish with spent lime half and mint sprig.

TED KILGORE, TASTE

What are the three key ingredients every bar should have? Fresh juice, bitters, and bourbon.

Your favorite appliance? Black & Decker juicer.

Which bars do you go to? Sanctuaria, Blood & Sand, and Demun Oyster Bar. I go where I know the bartender.

What is your favorite cocktail? I don't think I could ever choose between a classic martini and a Manhattan.

Kentucky Jewel

TED KILGORE, TASTE

SERVES 1

1 ½ ounce Buffalo Trace
  bourbon

½ ounce pineapple juice

½ ounce simple syrup

1 dash Angostura Bitters

Sparkling wine for topping

6 to 8 mint leaves

In shaker add all but wine. Add ice and shake for 20 seconds. Fine strain into cocktail glass and top with sparkling wine. Add mint garnish.

IN A PICKLE

TED KILGORE, TASTE

SERVES 1

1 ½ ounce Hendrick's gin

½ ounce St. Germain

½ ounce Velvet Falernum (rum-based liqueur)

¾ ounce lime

1 sprig dill

2 slices English cucumber

Shake and strain into a highball with a large rock. Garnish with an English cucumber slice and a small dill sprig.

MUIR ECOTINI

MATT McMULLIN, LOLA

SERVES 1

2 ounces 360 Peach Vodka

1 ounce Peach Schnapps

1 ounce Peach Nectar

Combine all of the ingredients in a cocktail shaker and shake to combine. Serve up in a martini glass.

RASPBERRY COLLINS

CHARLIE MYERS, McGURK'S PUBLIC HOUSE

SERVES 1

8 raspberries

2 ounces Plymouth Gin

¾ ounce fresh-squeezed lemon juice

¾ ounce simple syrup

1 ½ ounces club soda

Lemon wedge

Place 6 raspberries into a Collins glass and gently muddle until the juice is released. Fill the glass with ice, then add the gin, lemon juice and simple syrup and gently stir. Top off with the club soda. Garnish with a lemon wedge and remaining 2 raspberries.

PLYM AND TONIC

JAY OLSON, YA YA'S EURO BISTRO

SERVES 1

Sliced cucumber

1 ½ ounces Plymouth Gin

Tonic water

Rosemary sprig

Line a snifter with the sliced cucumber, then fill it with ice. Add the gin, then fill the glass with tonic water. Garnish with a rosemary sprig for stirring.

RASPBERRY-BASIL
LEMONADE

JAY OLSON, YA YA'S EURO BISTRO

SERVES 1

Sliced strawberries

Basil leaf, chiffonade cut

1 ½ ounces Bacardi light rum

5 ½ ounces lemonade

In a cocktail shaker, muddle the sliced strawberries with the basil. Add the rum and lemonade and stir to combine. Pour into an ice-filled highball glass.

Sister
Cities

taste with salt and pepper. Finish the soup by whisking in a touch of butter. Place a dollop of whipped crème fraîche in the center of each of 4 soup bowls. Divide the remaining ½ cup peas and the preserved lemon among the bowls, arranging them around the crème fraîche. Sprinkle the crushed pink peppercorns over the top. Pour the warmed soup around the crème fraîche and over the other ingredients at the table.

*Frozen, thawed and drained are fine

LANGOUSTINES, WARM GARLIC-CHAMPAGNE CREMA, AND POMEGRANATE

COLBY AND MEGAN GARRELTS, BLUESTEM, KANSAS CITY

SERVES 4

Langoustines are tiny lobsters that look like large prawns with pincers. Indigenous to Europe, fresh, unfrozen langoustines are extremely hard to get in the United States. If you can't order them, try to buy the largest shrimp you can find.

The pomegranate seeds in this recipe always surprise people at first. The scarlet kernels not only add a festive splash of color but also an unexpected crunch and a burst of juicy sweetness that brings out the fruitiness in the Champagne crema.

16 langoustines or extra-large shrimp

1 tablespoon vegetable oil

1 large shallot, minced

4 cloves garlic, finely chopped

1 ½ cups dry Champagne

1 cup heavy cream

1 tablespoon honey

1 large sprig fresh tarragon

2 tablespoons crème fraîche

Salt and freshly ground white pepper

5 tablespoons extra-virgin olive oil, divided

2 tablespoons butter, divided

¼ cup pomegranate seeds

1 ripe Bartlett pear, peeled, cored, and julienned

Zest of 1 lemon, finely sliced

Twist the pincers off the langoustines. Holding the head with one hand and the tail with another, gently twist and pull the head apart from the tail. Using kitchen shears, cut the underside of the tails. Pry open the shells and carefully pull out the tail meat in one piece. Save the heads, pincers, and shells for stock.

Make the crema: Heat the vegetable oil in a small saucepan over medium-high heat. Sauté the shallot and garlic until softened, about 3 minutes. Add Champagne and continue to cook until the mixture is reduced by half, about 5 minutes. Add the heavy cream, honey, and tarragon. Turn the heat down to medium-low and continue to simmer for 4 to 5 minutes.

Remove the saucepan from the heat. Discard the tarragon. Transfer the hot mixture to a blender and add the crème fraîche. Purée the crema until smooth. Season to taste with salt and pepper.

Heat 2 tablespoons of the olive oil in a large sauté pan over medium-low heat. Season the langoustines with salt and pepper. Roll the langoustine tails into balls. Working in two batches, sauté the langoustines in the oil for 30 seconds on each side. Add 1 tablespoon of the butter, remove the pan from the heat, and baste the langoustines with the melted butter for about 1 minute. Transfer the langoustines to a plate, tenting them with aluminum foil to keep warm. Pour the oil and butter out of the pan and repeat the process with the remaining oil, langoustines, and butter.

Toss the pear pieces with the remaining olive oil. Season with salt. Divide the langoustines and pomegranate seeds among 4 bowls. Spoon about ¼ cup of the Champagne crema over the langoustines. Top each bowl with some julienned pear and lemon zest. Serve immediately.

GRAHAM CRACKER POUND CAKE, HOT CHOCOLATE–POACHED PEARS AND BROWN BUTTER PECAN ICE CREAM

COLBY AND MEGAN GARRELTS, BLUESTEM, KANSAS CITY

SERVES 8

1 graham cracker pound cake (recipe follows)

Hot chocolate-poached pears (recipe follows)

Brown butter-pecan ice cream (recipe follows)

Slice the cake into 1-inch-thick slices. Place one slice of pound cake on each plate. Nest half of a warm poached pear next to each slice, and top each slice with a small scoop of brown butter-pecan ice cream. Serve immediately.

GRAHAM CRACKER POUND CAKE

1 cup (2 sticks) unsalted butter, softened

¾ cup sugar

¼ cup plus 1 tablespoon half-and-half

3 large eggs

2 teaspoons vanilla extract

¾ cup graham cracker crumbs

1 cup all-purpose flour

1 teaspoon baking powder

¼ teaspoon salt

Preheat the oven to 350 degrees. Generously butter an 8-by 4-inch loaf pan.

In the bowl of a stand mixer fitted with the paddle attachment, cream the butter and sugar together on medium-high speed until fluffy and light, scraping the bowl with a spatula as needed, about 15 minutes.

In a small bowl, whisk the half-and-half, eggs, and vanilla together. In a separate bowl, combine the graham cracker crumbs, flour, baking powder, and salt.

With the stand mixer on medium speed, add one-third of the wet ingredients to the creamed butter and mix until incorporated. Scrape down the bowl. With the stand mixer on low speed, add half of the dry ingredients and mix until incorporated. Repeat the process, alternating the wet and dry ingredients in thirds until everything is incorporated.

Transfer the batter to the loaf pan and bake for 60 to 65 minutes, or until a toothpick inserted in the middle of the loaf comes out clean. Let the cake cool completely on a wire rack.

HOT CHOCOLATE-POACHED PEARS

6 ½ cups water

2 ½ cups sugar

4 cinnamon sticks

1 teaspoon allspice berries

6 cloves

4 ounces bittersweet chocolate, chopped

2 ounces unsweetened chocolate, chopped

2 tablespoons plus 2 teaspoons unsweetened cocoa powder

4 tablespoons dark rum

2 pinches salt

4 semi-firm ripe pears, peeled, halved, and cored

This is a comforting and lovely alternative to wine poached pears. Letting the cooked pears steep in the chocolate poaching liquid overnight helps intensify the chocolate flavor. These pears are best served warm.

In a large saucepot, bring the water, sugar, cinnamon sticks, allspice, and cloves to a simmer over medium-high heat to dissolve the sugar. Add the chocolates, cocoa powder, rum, and salt and whisk until the chocolate is dissolved. Add the pears and poach them for 45 minutes over low heat. Turn them over halfway through the cooking process so they cook more evenly. They should be tender enough that a knife inserted in the thickest part will easily slip in and out.

Keep the pears warm until ready to serve. You may refrigerate the pears in their poaching liquid in an airtight container for up to 2 days. To reheat, warm the pears in their poaching liquid in a saucepan over medium-low heat.

BROWN BUTTER-PECAN ICE CREAM

- 6 egg yolks
- 2 cups heavy cream
- 1 cup whole milk
- ⅓ cup granulated sugar
- ⅓ cup packed light brown sugar
- ½ cup (1 stick) unsalted butter
- Pinch salt
- ½ cup toasted pecans, chopped

In a medium bowl, whisk the egg yolks together.

In a large saucepot, bring the cream, milk, and sugar to a low simmer over medium-high heat for 2 minutes or until the sugar has fully dissolved. Watch the pot closely, as it will boil over quickly.

Melt the butter in a sauté pan over medium heat. Once the foam subsides, watch the butter carefully. When the butter has browned (you will notice little dark specks in the butter), remove it from the heat. Stir the butter into the cream mixture; add a pinch of salt.

Temper the eggs by whisking 1 cup of the hot cream mixture into the yolks in a slow, steady stream. You want to add the hot cream slowly. Then combine the tempered eggs with the rest of the cream mixture.

Strain the ice cream base through a fine-mesh sieve into a large bowl. Set the bowl over ice and stir the ice cream base with a whisk until it has cooled slightly. Once the base has cooled, transfer it to an airtight container and refrigerate for at least 6 hours or overnight.

Churn the chilled base in an ice cream maker according to the manufacturer's instructions. Stir ½ cup chopped toasted pecans into the ice cream. Transfer the ice cream to a freezer-safe container. Freeze for at least 2 hours before serving.

DR PEPPER
SHORT RIBS

MIKE JALILI, TOUCH RESTAURANT, SPRINGFIELD

SERVES 4

I recommend making this a day early. It will taste better the next day.

- 4 short ribs
- Salt and pepper, to taste
- ½ cup olive oil
- 2 white onions, sliced
- Dr Pepper, enough to cover the ribs
- 1 cup red wine, preferably Syrah, Rhône, or Shiraz
- 3 celery stalks, chopped
- 3 carrots, chopped
- 6 tomatoes, quartered

Cut the fat off the ribs. Salt and pepper the ribs a little more than usual. In a Dutch oven, heat the olive oil. When it's very hot, add the ribs and sear on both sides until they are dark brown. Add the onions and cook for approximately 10 minutes. Add enough Dr. Pepper and red wine to cover the ribs and bring to boil. Add celery, carrots, and tomatoes and bring to a simmer. Cook a minimum of 6 to 8 hours, longer if needed, until the meat falls off of the bones.

INDEX

INDEX
BY CHEF

INDEX
BY RESTAURANT